The Prayer of David

The Prayer of David

In Times of Trouble

Michael D. Evans

Treasure House
An Imprint of
Destiny Image® Publishers, Inc.
P.O. Box 310
Shippensburg, PA 17257-0310

"For where your treasure is, there will your heart be also."
Matthew 6:21

ISBN 0-7684-3024-0

For Worldwide Distribution
Printed in the U.S.A.

This book and all other Destiny Image, Revival Press, MercyPlace, Fresh Bread, Destiny Image Fiction, and Treasure House books are available at Christian bookstores and distributors worldwide.

For a U.S. bookstore nearest you, call **1-800-722-6774**.
For more information on foreign distributors, call **717-532-3040**.
Or reach us on the Internet:
www.destinyimage.com

Contents

Preface

❧

Dear Reader,

Trouble is a state of worry or unrest caused by a person or a situation. Its goal is to force you to panic and place your faith in your circumstances rather than in God.

An amazing prayer changed the destinies of a terrified man, his family, and the world. I want to teach *YOU* to pray this prayer because it will make the same difference in your life—*IF you will read this little book and follow God's guidelines!* In the city of the birth of our Lord, Jerusalem, I began writing this transforming book about this amazing Prayer of David.

It is a prayer for victory *in the battles of life.*

All of the answered prayers of David are encapsulated in this amazing one-minute prayer, which ends, "May the Lord answer all of your prayers!" (Ps. 20:6, LB)

Since David's day, this prayer has been prayed over kings at their coronations. It was used as medicine during the Black Plague in Europe.

This prayer is truly a national anthem that is appropriate to sing at the outbreak of war for victory!

The Prayer of David is believed to have been used in public worship by the early church.

We know that our Lord read this psalm, His eyes beheld these words, and His lips spoke them, and I am sure that He prayed them.

David was an unlikely person to become the most blessed man in the entire Bible. This amazing prayer encompasses everything that David, you, or I could ever ask of God. The spotlight of Heaven was turned on, the hand of God moved, and the head of God turned as David prayed this prayer in faith!

David had to choose to believe that God was truly guiding his life, rather than choose to take matters into his own hands. The path of least resistance would have led to destruction for David, as it will in our lives. David had to get his eyes on Jehovah's promises and off his own predicament in order to live in peace. Peace was not the absence of conflict; it was having the courage to face the conflict and make the right choices. This was true in David's life; it is true in yours.

Revelation keys to a life of amazing favor are in this short intercessory prayer. The heart of David is supernaturally embodied in the Prayer of David. And God said David was a man after His heart...the heart that caused an unknown shepherd boy, considered in the eyes of his world a mere lump of clay, to become the cherished object of divine destiny.

The first thing to do in times of trouble: Trust God! When you do, you will find yourself abiding in the presence of God, as did David, who declared in Psalms 91 that you "shall not be afraid of...terror" (Ps. 91:5, NKJV). "He that dwelleth in the secret place of the most High shall abide under the shadow of the Almighty. I will say of the Lord, He is my refuge and my fortress: my God; in him will I trust" (Ps. 91:1-2, KJV). Once you place your trust in Him—not in self, not in others—you can pray the Prayer of David with faith, power, and authority. Then allow God to fight your battle.

If He did it for David, He will do it for you.

Join me now for *YOUR* life-changing revelation.

Michael David Evans

The Prayer of David

Jerusalem: The City of David
David Citadel

Chapter 1

FOR THOSE WHO DON'T HAVE A PRAYER!

❧

"In times of trouble, may the Lord respond to your cry!"

This little book in your hand is for people going through terrifying times, who really don't *feel* like they "have a prayer" of turning things around.

You have that prayer for them now!

The Prayer of David is a one-minute prayer.

God has answered this prayer time after time, and will do so again, and again, and again.

The only reason that the "Prayer of David" has not been answered more often is that it has been hidden.

In thirty-three years of ministry, I have never met one person who has ever prayed this amazing prayer.

Yet every word of the Bible was given by divine inspiration. In other words, God gave this prayer to David to pray.

That same God has given this prayer to you and me.

Get ready to plug your destiny into Heaven to turn your grief into glory!

From a Black Hole to a Holy Hill

David was a nobody in the world's eyes. Born on the wrong side of the tracks, David had no idea that the black hole he lived in would become, through the power of prayer, a holy hill.

A penniless, ignored boy would become one of the most prominent figures in the history of the world. He would become the most famous ancestor of Christ.

Jesus is not called the son of Abraham, or the son of Jacob, but the son of David.

David's story begins with God looking for someone to be anointed—someone through whom God could speak. David's nation needed to hear a word from the Lord. His nation was in crisis—just as our nation is in crisis now.

If you had said David's name, even the people in his tiny town of Bethlehem would have said, "David who?" When Samuel the prophet wanted to meet Jesse's sons so that he could anoint a king, Jesse didn't even acknowledge David as his son.

"Are all the young men here?" Samuel pressed. Jesse said that they were not: "There remains yet the youngest, and there he is, keeping the sheep" (1 Sam. 16:11, NKJV). *The youngest* meant "the insignificant one—not counting for very much." And to state that he was tending the sheep was a way of saying "*He has the job of a slave. Forget him!*"

The Lord was delighted with David. Delighted to the degree that He designated David's town as the spot where heaven and earth would meet at His birth.

David was proclaimed king, and anointed! Yet still he tended the sheep. The anointed king-to-be was the errand boy for his brothers, bringing them food and mail. The oldest got the inheritance of <u>Jesse</u>, yet the youngest of eight sons was going to get a <u>heavenly</u> inheritance beyond his wildest imagination.

You cannot choose to be a king; you are chosen. But true kingship is a total surrender to Christ's lordship.

Even after David was chosen by King Saul to be his armor-bearer, he still returned home to tend the sheep.

The Lord was delighted with David's dedication in handling his first assignment as a shepherd—*a job no one else wanted.* David's earthly father kept him believing that what he did was who he was.

So many of God's children believe lies. Those lies neutralize the magnificent plan and purpose God has for your life and leave a wake of depression, discouragement, and defeat. Believing a lie is as bad as telling a lie. Why? Because when we believe a lie, we accept fear as the norm. We put our faith in our fears. We crawl into a casket of self-pity and aren't even aware of it. The problem becomes our focus. Our eyes are not on the Lord; the problem becomes lord.

The ultimate goal of the father of lies is to father lies…seeds of doubt that choke out the Word. A lie will not only paralyze us from rejoicing in the victories of the past; it will cause us to hide from our destiny, surrendering to the enemy of our souls.

At His birth God chose to send an angel and a multitude of heavenly hosts to shepherds proclaiming, "There is born to you this day in the *City of David* a Savior which is Christ the Lord" (Lk. 2:11, KJV).

The Bright and Morning Star would place a star in the east as a sign of His coming.

David's name meant "favored"! He had no idea how greatly favored he was.

Mary, the mother of our Lord, would hear the words, "Highly favored, the Lord is with you" (Lk. 1:28, NIV). *You, too, are one of God's favorites. You will understand why as you read further.*

David's Bethlehem would never be the same and neither will where you live—whether it is a spiritual condition or a geographical location.

What you are reading is a life-changing revelation.

"For unto us a child is born, unto us a son is given: and the government shall be upon His shoulder: and his name shall be called Wonderful, Counsellor, the mighty God, the everlasting Father" (Is. 9:6, KJV).

David had no connections…no wealth…no status. He was a nobody on "God's road" to being a somebody. The heavenly spotlight of destiny was about to shine brightly on this young praying shepherd. No—God was not looking for a *somebody* with a big head.

He was looking for a nobody—with a praying heart.

David was unknown in Israel. His family was not in the register of the high and mighty.

No one wanted David's job—it was a dirty one.

Listen to David's prayer for *victory in battle*. You will understand why this prayer has been used over kings, as well as medicine during the Black Plague.

> *"In your day of trouble [or terror], may the Lord be with you. May the God of Jacob keep you from all harm! May He send you aid from His sanctuary in Zion. May He remember with pleasure the gifts you have given Him, your sacrifices and burnt offerings. May He grant you your heart's desire, and fulfill all your plans. May there be shouts of joy when we hear the news of your victory, flags flying with praise to our God for all that He has done for you. May the Lord answer all of your prayers!"* (Ps. 20:1-6, LB)

What do you do when financial, social or physical terror comes? Do you worry? Get angry and depressed? Withdraw?

Is God with you more, or less, in times of terror?

Do you blame Him?

Do you ask "God, how could You let this happen to me?"

Are you secretly mad at God?

Have you attended your own funeral…believing that your dreams have died?

The good news is, your dreams haven't died. It may be Friday—but Sunday's coming!

Are you expecting a miracle in times of terror? Your heart's desire is answered because of the seed you have sown. One seed, the seed of David, changed the world through Jesus Christ! Words are seeds, your time is a seed, and your offering is a seed.

You are a seed—your dreams are seeds—your plans are seeds.

What about your dreams and plans? Are you expecting them to come to pass when you are in times of terror? Or do you put them aside in discouragement?

"Mike, would you fly to the White House tomorrow? I need you to pray over a man. I'm sorry I can't tell you who he is."

"Sure, Carolyn," I said. Carolyn Sundseth was the religious liaison for then-President Ronald Reagan.

When I arrived at the White House, Carolyn said, "This is the man, Mike."

As I walked toward the man, a Scripture suddenly came to me. "Sir," I said, "you are going through trouble, but here is what God says: 'When you pass through the waters, I will be with you; and through the rivers, they shall not overflow you. When you walk through the fire, you shall not be burned, nor shall the flame scorch you'" (Is. 43:2, NKJV).

He looked at me as if I knew something about his trouble. I didn't, but God did! I left and flew to El Salvador, where I had a meeting with President Cristiani and a crusade in the San Salvador stadium.

When I picked up the morning paper in San Salvador, there on the front page was the man for whom I had prayed. His name was Oliver North. Years later he would tell me what that meeting meant to him.

"Mike," he said, "that Scripture was God-sent. From the Word you gave me that day years ago, I knew the Lord would deliver me. Thank you so much for caring."

At his time of literal trial and tribulation, Oliver North was about to be hung on a political cross as a scapegoat, but God delivered him. The end of the Oliver North story is a victorious one. He stood on the Word and believed that God would deliver him no matter how bad his situation looked.

There are similarities between David's and Oliver North's responses to dire straits. David stepped out of rejection into revelation! He stepped out of depression into delight. You have to step out to step up. When you place all of your worries in the hands of the Lord, you realize that it's not what you are going through that will determine your destiny and your disposition. It's when you open your eyes and see what you are going to! Like David, Oliver was able to see this because of the Word he took to heart.

Oliver North did not live in self-pity. And the greatest book of inspiration and encouragement ever written, the Psalms, was birthed out of the heart of a man who determined that he would not live in self-pity. David put his faith in the Lord in his times of terror, and he trusted God to answer his prayer. So did Oliver North. He rose above his circumstances because he knew his God was above them and would deliver him.

Are you excited knowing that all of Heaven is getting ready to have a celebration over *your* victory?

Why did the early church use the Twentieth through the Twenty-fourth Psalms in their worship?

It just hit me—"revelation determines reality!" What God reveals to you is reality!

The Prayer of David

King David said what God said! The words he spoke are the words of God—divinely inspired. He was saying what God says. He was praying what God says! You will be, too.

Praying the Word is saying the same thing that God says. It is much more powerful than what you or I say.

"I am going through a horrendous time of terror, Mike," you might say to me. I know—I have been there many times. But remember, "desperation is the mother of invention." If you're desperate, then you're hungry to do whatever it takes to change your situation.

Your life journey of praying the Word of God begins with the Twentieth Psalm.

Like the woman with the issue of blood who said, "If I may but touch His garment I shall be whole" (Mt. 9:20, KJV), you are going to transform your thinking through the power of the Word.

We see David praying a mighty prayer in desperation in the Twentieth Psalm.

We see David praising God after victory in battle in the Twenty-first Psalm!

"How the King rejoices in your strength, O Lord! How he exalts in Your salvation for You have given him his heart's desire; everything he asks you for! You welcome him to the throne with success and prosperity. You set a royal crown of solid gold upon his head. He asked for a long, good life, and You have granted his request; the days of his life stretch on and on forever. You have given him fame and honor. You have clothed him with splendor and majesty. You have endowed him with eternal

happiness. You have given him the unquenchable joy of your presence. And because the king trusts in the Lord, he will never stumble; never fall for he depends upon the steadfast love of the God who is above all gods. Accept our praise, O Lord, for all Your glorious power. We will write songs to celebrate Your mighty acts!"

David is saying what God says! He's praying what God says.

Yes, it's harvest time. If we will but believe God's words, we will not walk in fear.

"For God has not given us a spirit of fear, but of power, and of love, and of a sound mind" (2 Tim. 1:7, NKJV). I know what it is to walk in fear, and also to be delivered from fear.

Do you really believe that God is going to answer all of your plans?

If you don't—I understand. That was my story. But I assure you that if you join me in praying the Prayer of David daily, Heaven will leap in your direction. All of that doom and gloom will be gone forever!

In this little book, I am going to share with you a revelation on this prayer. If you stay with me, you will be hooked on God! May God smite you with hope...and may you never recover. That is my prayer for you.

My own story starts in a little school in the sixth grade. My history teacher, Mr. Morace, said, "Michael Evans, what do you want to be when you grow up?" All the other students had already raised their hands to announce their dreams.

"Twenty," I responded.

"No, Michael, what do you want to BE when you grow up?"

"Twenty," I said again. Everyone was laughing—I was so embarrassed.

The bell rang and school was out. I ran into the street crying, feeling like a nobody. Yes, I wanted to be *twenty* when I grew up. Not a doctor or a lawyer—just twenty (years old). I had begun running away from home at age four. I never got far, and most of the time my parents never knew I was gone. I had nowhere to run and always went home.

At age four I was running hard with no shoes on. I could have gone six or eight blocks until I got to the park. It was a cool fall day. The leaves were evermore. Wheelchairs were lined up, and old people from a nursing home were throwing breadcrumbs to the pigeons. "Here, little boy," a big lady from the nursing home said, "feed the pigeons."

"No," I cried as I threw down the breadcrumbs and ran. "I don't want to feed the pigeons." I realize now that what I was really saying was "I don't like myself, I don't like my circumstances, and I don't feel loved or special. I don't like this town—I don't want to end up in a wheelchair someday feeding the pigeons with no purpose for my life. I don't want to just be a kid who lived in the projects, doomed to a life of trouble."

I was sure that my father hated me. A few days before the nightmare scenario when my teacher asked me what I wanted to be when I grew up, my father came into my room in a drunken rage. He grabbed me by the throat and threw me high into the air. I hung on to his hands, trying desperately to get free from his vise-like grip. Panic hit me. I could feel my urine running down my legs—then blackness. When I awoke on the floor, I smelled the sickening stench of vomit. I had vomited all over myself. My father's finger marks were still on my neck.

When I was older, there was no way I would tell the teacher at school about my home life. One time, in gym, the other kids and teachers saw my bloodstained black and blue legs, scarred from being beaten by extension cords and coat hangers. They came to my house and talked to my father. I had never told them that my father had done these things, but he didn't believe me. He beat me until I was hysterical and threw me in a canning cellar with a dirt floor. I vowed then never to let a teacher know anything.

I hated Fridays. My mother couldn't drive, and I walked with her to the A & P grocery store to buy groceries. I would push the shopping cart home.

We experienced discrimination first hand. People would scream at us, and sometimes they would throw tomatoes or eggs.

"Why do they hate us?" I asked.

"Oh, all Christians hate Jews. They think we crucified Christ. Russian Orthodox Christians killed your great-grandfather, burning him to death in Russia. The German Christians gassed many of my relatives in Germany and even made lampshades from their skin. The Pope, Billy Graham and Adolf Hitler were all Christians. Jesus died, Michael. Don't ever try to dig him up." This story was told to me time and time again.

That Friday night would live in my heart forever. At around 1:50 a.m. I awoke. Hearing screaming, I ran to the stairs. My mother was sitting next to my father. He was screaming "You whore! Tell me about that bastard, Michael," as he punched her in the face. I cried in pure agony. My mother was suffering so, and it was all my fault. I ran, wet with tears, into my room, and sat on the side of the bed crying. It seemed like I spent an eternity with my hands over my face.

"God, why was I born?" I cried out in desperation.

Suddenly I sensed that a bright light was on in that dark hole of a room. I felt warm all over and knew it wasn't my father. I didn't hear a sound. My heart was beating a mile a minute. I peeked through my fingers to look. There before me two hands were extended, and in the centers of the hands were nail scars.

"How can this be?" I thought. "This can't be Jesus. He's dead!" I remember what was going on in my mind as I lifted my head higher and lowered my hands.

"Oh my God! It is Jesus." I felt such peace as I looked into His smiling eyes. They were amazing. Every color in the rainbow was in those eyes. I have never seen such happy eyes. I could see through them. I saw angels and beauty beyond description.

His mouth opened and He said, "Son, I love you and have a great plan for your life." Just as soon as He came, He left. I had never heard those three wonderful words from my earthly father—ever.

That was forty-three years ago. No, I have not *seen* Him since, but that night changed my life forever. The

Lord responded to my cry and I was healed of a speech impediment, a stomach ulcer, and was delivered from all my fears. I know they were in the hundreds.

I was gloriously saved. Hope filled my soul like a tidal wave. That hope has never left.

I don't think the Lord was in my room more than a minute—the very room where my father had almost killed me just days before. *But that one minute changed my life forever.*

One word from God, one touch from God, will change your life forever.

If my prayer had not been answered, you would not be reading this little book. I am sure I would have been dead by twenty—if not by my father's hands, then by my own. The amazing thing is that I *have* experienced the hand of God on me as I have stood on a promise as strongly as I did when our Lord appeared to me on October 13, 1958.

My terrors began at a very young age:

- Depression

- Discouragement

- Defeat

I thought I deserved all the bad things that were happening to me. I thought God was mad at me. Prayer has destroyed the power of the demonic lie for me. It will for you, too, if you dare to join me in praying the Prayer of David. Pray it daily. As you do, watch the mighty explosion of God in your life.

As I write this little book, my beautiful wife of thirty-three years, my married daughters and sons-in-law, and my son, Michael David, are gathered in our home to celebrate the birth of our Lord that took place long ago in David's little town of Bethlehem.

Why not call the book *The Prayer of King David*? Because you may not relate to a king. I met a king once—King Carlos of Spain. He only had time to say, "Hello. How are you?" Before I could respond, he turned to the next person and said the same thing. The good news is that by the time this little book is finished, you **will** be able to relate to a king.

I always secretly wanted a son to love, probably because I never had a dad who loved me. I thought I would have only girls, which was fine. They are my sweethearts! But God gave Carolyn and me a gift. When our son was born, Carolyn said, "Honey, I want to name him after you." I knew that was a problem. She wanted to name him Michael David Evans II, but I didn't have a middle name. Well, you guessed it. I went to a judge to get my name changed to Michael David Evans I. I tell my son, "I was named after you. When I grow up I want to be just like you."

So I'm a David, and so are hundreds of thousands of average people around the world. I wanted this book to be *my book, your book, our book*. I want us to uncover principles that will light our fire and send us heavenward in our journey in life, with joy unspeakable and full of glory.

Over the years, I have traveled millions of miles speaking to more than four thousand audiences, from the Kremlin Palace in Moscow to the Royal Palace in Madrid…touching the lives of presidents, kings, and prime ministers. Everything Christ promised in my prayer has come to pass. He indeed has done it. That's why I'm so excited about this revelation of the Prayer of David.

God answers prayer...not only King David's prayers, but yours and mine too.

Praying the Word is a lost art in Christianity. Why pray a prayer that someone else prayed? Because the "someone" we are talking about received that prayer from God Almighty. Through the Holy Spirit, as you pray the Prayer of David, you are praying a Holy Spirit, heavenly prayer sent from God and recorded in the Bible. This prayer is a word from God.

One word from God can change your life forever.

I joined the Army at seventeen on the buddy system. My best friend (dog tag number RA112051) was shot dead by a sniper. My tag was RA112052. God saved my life!

I have been in many hellholes in my life's journey:

- Hellholes of emotion

- Hellholes of finance

- Hellholes of geography

- Hellholes of the spirit

In all of these places I would have been killed if God had not answered my prayer. I have always stood on a promise from the Word and made it a prayer. But no promise has had a greater impact on my life than the Prayer of David. I know that David was given this prayer by the spirit of God—it was not his own. He prayed what God told him to pray. You and I can also.

HE ONLY NEEDS TO SEE YOU

No, you don't have to see Jesus to have your prayers answered. He only needs to see you. There is no communication system to contact Him except prayer. Praying the Word is the highest form of prayer. You can't pray the Word without your faith growing. Praying in faith can activate the angels of Heaven and transform ordinary people into giant-killers to shake nations.

Praying this prayer, I have seen the fruit of it in my own life. It is my prayer that the Prayer of David will ignite faith in your heart as you join me in praying it daily. So that together we might hear what He hears and see what He sees, so that we might do what He does!

"Do you pray the Word?" I asked Mother Teresa when we were in Rome on the way to Jerusalem.

"Every day," she said, smiling. "Prayer makes our hearts bigger until they are capable of containing the gifts of God Himself."

I shared with her my vision for revival and healing in the City of David.

"I will join you in praying for healing among God's children in the Holy Land," she said. Then she took my hand and we prayed together—it was joy unspeakable and full of glory.

I have prayed this Prayer of David in many of the hellholes of the world:

- Iraq

- Cambodia

- Beirut

- Somalia

God has always heard and answered this prayer.

The Lord revealed His plan and Himself to David. *Why? David had failed God and committed adultery, even murder. He was far from perfect.*

It was not David's sin that drew God to him, but rather David's hungry passion to touch God in prayer. A hungry heart surrendering to the lordship of eternity triggered a heavenly response.

David's story is one of a man's face bronzed by the hot heat of adversity. But he had a heart that was bursting with holy delight, knowing that his Lord was always more than able to deliver him in times of terror.

David found the entrance into the presence of God. God was so pleased with him that the Lord allowed David's fingerprints to be everywhere. God's extravagant love affair with David was the reason for his season. It is also the reason for your season.

A little shepherd boy would become the most famous king of Israel and reign in the City of David— Jerusalem—a few miles from the hills of Bethlehem.

It was a new day for David. Why not let this be the first day of the rest of your life?

Someone said, "If you do what you've always done, you'll have what you've always had."

Why not make a wholehearted commitment to get out of a rut? Let the power of praying the Word carry you into a realm of transforming faith where you will never be the same.

David did indeed touch God in such a way that the world would never be the same.

You can, too, so that your world will never be the same.

"*The steps of a good man are ordered by the Lord: and he delighteth in his way. Though he fall, he shall not be utterly cast down: for the Lord upholdeth him with his hand*" (Ps. 37:23-24, KJV). David knew that it was impossible to walk with God without having a hungry, devoted heart.

I am praying the Prayer of David with the same determination that I prayed "God, why was I born?"

And I'm expecting a miracle. I don't think I will see Jesus again, as I did at the age of eleven, until I see Him in Heaven. But I don't need to...I see Him in His Word. It's all over me, and it's keeping me alive.

God was getting ready to anoint what David had. And He is getting ready to anoint what you have.

David was able to defeat the enemies of his soul because he allowed God to define who he was and what he was.

David prayed this prayer with a desperate hungry heart. He knew that prayer was his only way out.

**He knew that God knew his name,
his nature and his need.**

The New Testament begins with Jesus Christ, the descendant of King David.

It ends with, "I am the Root and the Offspring of David, the Bright and Morning Star" (Rev. 22:16, NKJV).

David's God was a good God. And so is yours.

"For I know the thoughts that I think toward you, says the Lord, thoughts of peace and not of evil, to give you a future and a hope" (Jer. 29:11, NKJV).

God indeed gave David a future and a hope. How? By answering David's prayers!

As you read this little book, learn the revelation of the Prayer of David.

"May the Lord answer all of your prayers!" (Ps. 20:6, LB)

Your life journey of praying the words of God begins with the Twentieth Psalm.

Chapter 2

THE MIGHTY WARRIOR IS WAITING

∽

"May the Lord respond to your cry. May the God of Jacob keep you safe from all harm!"

I had just finished preaching at Earl's Court in London. Evander Holyfield, the heavyweight champion of the world, had flown in to share his testimony in the meeting. Afterward, we went out to eat together.

"Evander, tell me about your last fight with Mike Tyson," I said.

"Mike, I was in big trouble. My sparring partner was beating me. I was not ready to fight Tyson. I just could not get it together no matter how hard I tried. I needed the Lord's help. Tyson was going to knock my block off if I did not get help fast. I knew I was going into harm's way, high speed!

"I went to my wife, Janice. She is a woman of God who knows how to pray, and I asked her, 'Did God tell you anything for me? I need help bad.'

"'Yes,' Janice said. 'The Lord said He would give me a song, and when you sing it the spirit of the Lord would come on you.'

"'Where is it?' I said. 'I need it now.'

"'Sorry, the Lord hasn't given it to me yet,' she told me.

"Days went by and then a week. I was getting real worried. Where's the song?" Evander asked, as he reflected back on the real concern he had before the fight. "Finally, one day Janice came in and said, 'Here's the song, mighty warrior.'"

Evander continued to tell me that it was a song about King David. It talks about dancing like David dances...singing like David sang.

Evander said, "When I heard it, the power of God hit me. I ran through the house shouting. I decided to have MGM play it as I came out so everyone could lift Jesus up. As I was getting my hands taped a reporter stuck his head in my dressing room and said, 'This battle is between Muhammad and Jesus. Who's going to win?'

"I liked that. I knew who had already won that battle. Tyson was Muslim.

"As I started to the floor, the black pastor of a little church said, 'Evander, God told me you need to protect your face in the third round. Yes, you will win, but protect your face in the third round.'

"Well, I thought maybe Tyson would try to head butt me or try to catch me off guard. I had no idea he was going to try to bite my ear off. But PTL," said Evander, as he pointed heavenward, "the mighty warrior won the fight."

Evander made Jesus Lord. He totally trusted Him with his gift and God blessed him.

David's prayer was "I am in trouble." *In the Hebrew* trouble *means "in times of worry"! In times of terror, we only have to choose to walk in fear and worry or walk in faith and rejoice while standing on the Word.*

God does not want us to worry. We are admonished to pray about everything, and the God of peace will keep our hearts and minds in Christ Jesus!

David was in big trouble. He had gone after flesh rather than the Lord, and committed adultery with Bathsheba. When she told him "I am with child," David sent word to Joab to have her husband, Uriah the Hittite, killed. (See Second Samuel chapter 11.)

God sent Nathan to David with the word. "You are the man" (2 Sam. 12:7, NKJV).

David needed to see the footprints of the Savior to cover his flesh prints of sin.

David was terrified. He had covered his sin for about a year, living in deception and hypocrisy. Then Nathan showed up and cancelled the building permit. David was not going to be allowed to build the Temple. Instead, judgment was on the way. David repented and cried out to God with a sincere heart. Yes, he was in big trouble.

David realized that he would not be winning any battles. While he was on the throne, he needed to be a sheep, and needed Adonai, the Lord, to be his shepherd. David wanted to play with God, but he forgot that God was going to show up and play with him!

It is not what we do that defines who we are, it is who we are that defines what we do.

When we surrender our hearts fully to the lordship of the God of Jacob, then the "who" abiding in us will determine what we do.

David needed help, badly. And he got it. He was the first king to unite Israel.

The first king to receive the promise of a royal Messiah in his line.

David knew that shepherds were responsible for guidance and provision, yet he needed the guidance and provision of the Lord to succeed. And he got it.

David was a shepherd king, but he wanted a Shepherd King over his life. David knew he needed to surrender his control and ownership. David chose to turn the ownership of his life over to the Great Shepherd. David knew the only hope in his time of terror was to respond to the rights and authority of the Lord and follow His direction. He had to come to the place of being utterly content with the Lord's management of his life.

You may not be in the kind of trouble that David was, but all trouble is trouble. Trouble is relative to your own personal situation, circumstances, and problems. If you have one million dollars, and you lose it all, you are broke; if you have one thousand dollars, and you lose it all, you are broke; if you have one hundred dollars, and you lose it all, you are broke. In each case, you are in trouble.

No matter what the circumstance, we need to surrender completely to the Lord.

Jesus said, "I am the good shepherd: the good shepherd giveth his life for the sheep" (Jn. 10:11, KJV)!

Isaiah the prophet declared:

"All we like sheep have gone astray, we have turned every one to his own way; and the Lord hath laid on him the iniquity of us all" (Is. 53:6, KJV).

Outside of Jesus being Lord, we are under the authority of the god of this world.

I spent eleven days in the Sinai desert. I climbed Mount Sinai by starlight with a young shepherd guiding me. In the desert, there are flies everywhere. Big flies! The sheep are plagued by the flies that get in their noses. The sheep butt their heads against trees, rocks, and posts to try to keep the flies from bothering them.

"Why all the erosion?" I asked the little shepherd as we were climbing Sinai.

"Sheep have traveled this way and made ruts and gullies. They also dig at the roots of the vegetation, killing it, and the sheep are starving now. This happened because shepherds were lazy and the sheep had no direction. The shepherds must keep the sheep moving to prevent this from happening," he responded.

He revealed his solution. "I dip my sheep in olive oil, sulfur, and spices and don't have a problem with the flies." Satan is called "beelzebub," lord of the flies.

When we surrender to the Lord, all rivalry goes…all selfishness goes…all stubbornness goes. We can say, "The Lord is my shepherd; I shall not want" (Ps. 23:1, KJV).

When the Lord responds to our cry, He is with us. We are at peace in Him. But He cannot respond to our cry if we are on the throne of our lives.

May the God of Jacob keep you safe from ALL harm.

Jacob's God was a God of grace! Jacob deserved judgment, but God showed him mercy.

Jacob was a flawed man. His faults and failures were known to everyone in town.

David drew strength from knowing Jacob's faults. He thought, *Maybe, if God used Jacob, He will use me.*

God revealed Himself in a personal way to Jacob. David desperately needed a touch from a personal God.

David needed a refuge! God defended Jacob against all—even those in his own family.

David needed ***that*** God to be ***his*** refuge.

"God is our refuge and strength, a very present help in trouble....The Lord of hosts is with us; the God of Jacob is our refuge" (Ps. 46:1,7, KJV).

Calling him the God of Jacob signifies that the covenant God is coming. God cut covenant with Jacob, making him heir of Abraham's faith and Isaac's promise.

In Middle Eastern culture, the *guest* has a place of honor. To this day, the *host is responsible to protect the guest.*

You are the Lord's guest. You are in His tent (tabernacle) and He is obliged by His covenant to keep you from all harm.

The Hebrew meaning of *New Testament* is "new covenant."

Disciples were called in the Hebrew "Hassids," or **covenant keepers.** *Paul wrote letters to the covenant keepers in:*

- Galatia

- Ephesus

- Corinth

A covenant is a contract when two are in agreement.

Psalms declares, "How good and how pleasant it is for brethren to dwell together in unity!" (Ps. 133:1, KJV)

Unity is a wonderful Hebrew word...*echod.*

It is in the oldest prayer in Judaism: "Hear, O Israel, the Lord our God, the Lord is *echod* [One]."

The verb is found in the book of Joel:

"Your sons and your daughters shall *chazzah* [prophesy]" (Joel 2:28, KJV).

When we are in covenant with God and with our self and with His body, prophecy power (*chazahel*) is released.

The Bible says, "Now the God of peace, that brought again from the dead our Lord Jesus, that great shepherd of the sheep, through the blood of the everlasting covenant, make you perfect in every good work to do his will, working in you that which is wellpleasing in his sight, through Jesus Christ; to whom be glory forever and ever. Amen" (Heb. 13:20-21, KJV).

We are safe from all harm through the power of the blood of the Lamb!

When Samuel went to Bethlehem to offer a sacrifice to God, he took blood and oil and touched the four extremities as a symbol of purification, as was the custom for a prophet or priest when offering a sacrifice.

Jesus the Lamb of God was pierced through all four extremities. *When we are in His hands and know it, we will say it boldly in prayer.*

A shepherd is responsible for *provision— guidance—and protection*.

He takes care of his sheep.

Jacob's God was also a personal God. Jacob needed to be touched by God and he was. Jacob's name was changed to Israel.

David was not in the priesthood nor had he been ordained as a priest, but God made him one.

"But you shall be to me a kingdom of priests!" (Rev. 1:6)

When He is Lord, He keeps you safe from all harm! Because you are His!

A priest presents a person to God or presents God to a person. A priest makes a God-connection.

"When the chief Shepherd shall appear, ye shall receive a crown of glory that fadeth not away" (1 Pet. 5:4, KJV).

Jesus said, "I am the good shepherd: the good shepherd giveth his life for the sheep" (Jn. 10:11, KJV).

Now in the revelation of the crucifixion, the Shepherd King proclaims the power of the cross in Psalm 23:

"Because the Lord is my Shepherd, I have every- thing I need! He lets me rest in the meadow grass and leads me beside the quiet streams. He gives me new strength. He helps me do what honors Him the most. Even when walking through the dark valley of death, I will not be afraid, for thou are close beside me, guiding me all the way. You provide deli- cious food for me in the presence of my enemies.

You have welcomed me as your guest; blessings overflow me. Your goodness and unfailing kindness shall be with me all of my life, and afterwards I will live with you forever in your home."

David's physical weapon in the field was a patch of leather, two pieces of braided twine, and smooth stones, along with a rod and a staff. He used his weapons against the enemy. David would twirl the sling over his head and let go of one end of the twine. David knew how to protect his sheep, and the Lord—the Good Shepherd—knows how to keep His sheep safe, also.

The shepherd David wanted the Lord to be his Shepherd. He wanted the Lord to know him by name as David knew each of his sheep by name. He wanted the Lord to protect and care for him just as he protected and cared for his sheep. David never left the sheep. He was not a part-time shepherd.

I met a shepherd in the desert who slept at the entrance of a cave. His body became the door. Another shepherd led his flock into a circular, rocky area and lay down at the entrance. The wolves would have to go over the shepherd to get to the sheep.

David had learned to trust the Chief Shepherd of his soul. He believed the Good Shepherd would hold him as David held the delicate young lambs in the fields of Bethlehem. When the wolves are circling, what do you do…panic and run, or trust the Good Shepherd? *"My sheep hear My voice, and I know them, and they follow Me.*

And I give them eternal life, and they shall never perish; neither shall anyone snatch them out of My hand" (Jn. 10:27-28, NKJV).

David was a *God-worshiper*.

God's voice was more real to him than the voice of the enemy, be it a lion or a bear or a giant.

"Faith comes by hearing, and hearing by the word of God" (Rom. 10:17, NKJV). Pray David's prayer and let your faith grow. *The reason David could kill Goliath was that his faith was greater than Israel's fear.*

Who or what is your Goliath? What is sucking the energy right out of you…terrorizing you at night…at home…on the job…at school…in your mind? David defeated his Goliath "in the name of the Lord of hosts, the God of the armies of Israel" (1 Sam. 17:45, KJV). David knew as he met Goliath in the Valley of Blood that the battle was between righteousness and evil. He knew that the battle was the Lord's, and in order to have power with God, David would have to lose all faith in the flesh! He committed himself to the King of kings to be owned, possessed by royalty.

When you truly believe you are anointed and appointed, you will pass on what you have, no matter what the circumstances.

David not only knew that the battle was the Lord's; he knew how to encourage himself in the Lord even in the most unjust of days. David was a God-pleaser! He refused to worship the gods of wood and stone…the gods of sex and power. David knew that flesh could not inherit the kingdom of God, no matter what the cause! Man-pleasers always see giants in the Promised Land, never the Promised Land in them.

Goliath was the seed, the offspring, of the giants that the spies saw when they went into the Promised Land. The children of Israel looked on the size of the giants and said, "We are not able" (Num. 13:31, NKJV). But Caleb and Joshua looked on the size of their God, and knew they were more than able!

Is the battle the Lord's, or do you fight it? Listen to what comes from your mouth. Are you betrayed by your words? Are you negotiating with the enemy or trusting in God? "There is a way that seems right to a man, but in the end it leads to death" (Prov. 16:25, NIV). The only way to win the battle is God's way.

What has happened to your vision? Has it died? David never gave up on God. He knew that God would do His part. David had no fear of the giant in his life. God-pleasers are not afraid of "the arrow that flies by day" (Ps. 91:5, NKJV).

David was mistreated, hurt, and painfully rejected. The enemy wanted to keep David dwelling on the pain of his past. He could have developed a "why me" mentality, but he did not sit around in defeat or discouragement. He knew he was born to be a warrior in the midst of a nation with a slave mentality…a nation defeated by a giant, Goliath. David encouraged himself in the Lord. He did not spend his time with negative people who would make attempts to discourage him, telling him it was hopeless.

David knew that through the power and authority of God, he would defeat Goliath, and drive the enemy out of his land, his mind, his emotions. He defeated his

Goliath, and there would be no rematch. He proclaimed boldly, "Is there not a cause?" (1 Sam. 17:29, KJV) But just because David was anointed king did not mean that Saul would step aside and relinquish the throne. While Saul remained on the throne, David had to believe that God would do what He said He would do.

David determined in his heart that he would be a man of prayer and put God's words above his own. You cannot fight a spiritual battle with physical weapons. David was willing to pay the price, even sacrificing his pride, his ego, and his desires. This would determine his success.

David understood that what he was willing to make happen for others through his obedience, God would make happen for him. David's significance as a man-king would be determined by his servant's spirit to a God-King. He knew that only in dying to his desires would he see the glory of the Living God. His connection with eternal kingship would flourish based on his focus during the storms of life on the King of kings.

You must not worry about what people think as long as you are consumed with what God thinks. Hell does not have a knife sharp enough to slice through the heavenly armor in which God desires to clothe you.

David's praise to Jehovah became a sacrifice in the dark, private hours of his life. That sacrifice of praise offered in secret would become the measuring rod for what a God-King would give to David in the public arena.

If you truly believe that the Bible is the Word of God and is anointed by God, then you understand how David's praying of Psalms 20, with a high priority for the spirit of God, caused this revelation to open to him. These are not the words of a man. *They are the words of Father God.*

One word from God changed David's life forever, and it will change yours also! *That word from God is before your eyes right now.* Believe it!

Chapter 3

HELP IS ON THE WAY

"May He send you help from His sanctuary in Zion, and strengthen you from Jerusalem."

Why does God resist the proud but give grace to the humble? Because the proud person does not ask for help—not even God's.

The shepherd boy of Bethlehem is now the king of Jerusalem. Today is a calendar day. David is bringing the ark of God to Jerusalem. Jehovah is going to be the center of Jerusalem. David is going to proclaim Him Lord and King! *Help is on the way.* (See Second Samuel 6:12-15;17-19.)

David knew that when God fought for Israel, the Israelites won every battle!

Sanctuary for the believer—if he chooses to abide there—is in God's presence.

Where is His sanctuary? Now He resides in the believer.

David got more revelation about God, and from God, in the Psalms, than anyone else in the entire Bible, except our Lord. David was the most:

- excited,

- enthusiastic,

- exuberant,

- delighted, and

- dynamic

worshiper in the entire Bible. It didn't happen by accident. David had to get his prayer answered in his time of trouble to break through into revelation and joy unspeakable, full of glory.

David stepped out of rejection into revelation! He stepped out of depression into delight. You have to step out to step up.

When you place all of your worries in the Lord's hands, you realize that it's not what you're going through that will determine your destiny and your disposition. *It's when you open your eyes and see what you are going to!!*

The greatest book of inspiration and encouragement ever written, the Psalms, was birthed out of the heart of a man who determined that he would not live in self-pity, but would put his faith in the Lord in his times of terror, and trust God to answer his prayer.

David could not sit around playing the "blame game" waiting for life to be fair and others to fight his battles. He had to stand up like a warrior in the midst of adversity and encourage himself in the Lord. David could not rely on others for his victory, and neither can we. As long as we are lethargic, indifferent, and having a "pity party" while blaming others, we will never fulfill our destiny. A warrior mentality does not exempt us from difficult circumstances, or even setbacks. What it does cause us to do is to arise to a new height. It will cause us to realize that the past is dead, as God said to Joshua, "Moses, my servant, is dead. Arise....Every place the soles of your feet touch, I will give it unto you" (Joshua 1:2,3).

What has God promised you? Do you have a vision for victory for your life? If you will speak the promises of God, meditate on His Word, and determine that you will allow nothing...nothing, to keep you from becoming everything God has created you to be, then you will, indeed, develop a warrior spirit. You will stand against the forces of darkness, look them squarely in the face, and encourage yourself in the Lord. David, in the midst of adversity, heard the Lord tell him he would pursue, overtake, and recover all (see 1 Sam. 30:8). And so will you!

The Bible says, "The people that do know their God shall be strong, and do exploits" (Dan. 11:32, KJV). God did not choose King David to live in this end-time hour, but He has chosen you. Refuse defeat! Guard your words. Encourage yourself in the Lord.

Remember that you are guaranteed victory from the creator of the universe because of what our Lord did at Calvary. You have to rise up and fight the fight of faith.

"In him we live and move and have our being" (Acts 17:28, NKJV). We reside in Him. God is our "very present help in trouble" (Ps. 46:1, KJV).

"Don't worry, Maureen, help is on the way!" As I turned, I thought, "What have you just said?" The lady was Maureen Reagan Revell. She and her husband Dennis had just returned from a fact-finding mission meeting with African presidents for her father, President Ronald Reagan. I had a dream to go to Africa and hold great crusades.

The Lord had told me to go to Mexico to the Princess Hotel in Acapulco and pray for two days. On the second day I was outside praying when a couple walked by.

The Lord spoke to my spirit. "Ask her if you can help her resolve the president's great need in Africa."

"Lord, she doesn't know me, and I don't even know who she is," I said to the Lord. I didn't find out who the woman was until I told her what God had related to me. It was then that she introduced herself and her husband. She was Maureen Reagan, daughter of our president.

Well, I have learned that I can never win an argument with the Lord, so I obeyed and asked her if I could help her. Her response was one that I should have expected because of the God we serve.

"Yes, you can. There is a new president in Uganda. He wants to speak to the U.S. broadcasters. I can't arrange a big meeting; can you?" Maureen asked me.

"Yes, tell him help is on the way! I will call Dr. Ben Armstrong, the executive director of the National Religious Broadcasters, and ask him if he will allow President Museveni to speak."

Dr. Armstrong said "Yes." Later, what a joy it was for me to host President Museveni's cabinet in my suite at the Washington Hilton Hotel.

Museveni rededicated his life to Christ in that meeting and invited me to Uganda. His secretary of state became my crusade coordinator for Africa. God is amazing!

When we trust Him instead of our human reasoning, great things can happen.

The flesh refuses to trust in God. Instead the flesh life trusts in stuff, in people, and in self. David could say, "been there, done that—no thanks."

As I sat in the Dallas/Fort Worth Airport writing this chapter while waiting for my flight, I noticed a security guard. The Lord impressed me to speak to her.

"Stop what you're doing and tell her 'Help is on the way.' Tell her that 'she is blessed and highly favored' and that God is not mad at her."

Tears streamed down her face as I shared the Word that the Lord had placed in my spirit.

"Mike, my mother just died. She was a godly woman, as was my grandmother. I rebelled against them. I have three children and no husband—no food or gifts for the kids for Christmas. But I told the Lord I would put Him first and two days later I got this job. I'm so grateful."

"Well," I said, "so am I." I handed her money to buy food and presents for her kids. She broke down crying with joy. She said, "I thought God was mad at me! That was a lie, wasn't it? Yes, it was. I will get in church Sunday."

"Where should I go?" she then asked me. After giving her some directions, I went on my way. She ran up to the plane and said, "God bless this man of God."

Do we need help? Do we need to be strengthened? Yes! Yes! Yes!

The root word for Jerusalem means "inheritance, estate." Our God desires to send us help and strengthen us from His abundant estate, and our inheritance through His shed blood.

Angels came straight from Heaven's sanctuary to strengthen our Lord.

I have found that God intentionally allows us to exhaust ourselves when we are operating in our own strength.

We must wake up and realize that only He can provide the strength we need.

One morning in prayer I heard the words in my spirit, "Go to Jerusalem. What you do will affect the destiny of the nation." I contacted twelve partners, told them what God had told me, and asked them to meet me there.

The night before they were to arrive I became greatly troubled.

"Lord, I don't know what we're here for. I can't tell these people I'm taking them on a tour—they really believe in me, and that you have sent us here for a divine purpose! What am I here to do?"

"Go to sleep," I sensed the Lord saying.

While I slept, I had a dream. I saw the man on a platform with me saying, "Thank you for coming. The reason we are here is…" and nothing came out of my mouth. I tried it again: "The reason we are here is …" and the same thing happened. It really shook me.

Finally, in the dream, I started for the door to get out of there. Suddenly I saw an angel as big as the door. He shouted, "The key to the mission is Zerubbabel 4:6." I awoke from my sleep and opened my Bible to Zechariah chapter 4.

Our group of twelve ended up in the house of Prime Minister Begin, praying over him. I asked everyone to join hands. Then we prayed for a general by the name of Sharon, who is now Israel's prime minister. We prayed for many generals that week. Charles Duke, one of the Apollo mission astronauts, began weeping and asking forgiveness of an Israeli general.

Charles shared with the general that on a trip to the moon, he found Jesus Christ, and "He forgave me of all my sins. I was anti-Semitic and I must confess this to you and ask forgiveness."

The news broke forty-eight hours after I arrived home. The phone rang, and it was the senior advisor to the prime minister. "Mike, I have great news. War broke out in Lebanon, and we shot down ninety Russian MIGS and twenty-five hundred SAM missiles without losing a plane. *It is a miracle. Thank the men for coming and praying over our leaders. God has answered that prayer.*"

I hurried back and told the partners to turn to the book of Zerubbabel, the fourth chapter, the sixth verse. This verse was the key to the mission. Well, I'm sure you've figured it out—there is no book of Zerubbabel. I then said, "Men, I don't know what to do. I only know that the Lord said come." At that the angel shouted "Zechariah." I alone saw the angel and heard the words. I immediately turned to Zechariah 4 and began reading.

Then the angel woke me from my dream.

He asked me, as if I had been asleep, "Do you know what you see?"

"No, I don't," I said.

So he said to me, "This is the word of the Lord to Zerubbabel: 'Not by might nor by power, but by my Spirit,' says the Lord Almighty" (Zech. 4:6, NIV).

Help is on the way! No matter what you're going through:

- Emotionally

- Physically

- Financially

- Socially

- Legally

Help is on the way if you will put your trust in God's power. God really does understand where we are in our situations, circumstances and trials. He sees our "black holes" of poverty, grief, abuse, neglect, unhappiness, and malaise in life.

At nineteen years of age I was living in downtown Philadelphia. It was my last year in the Army, and the pay wasn't much...around three hundred dollars a month. I came into town after visiting my folks and parked my car in a parking garage. I gave the attendant an extra five-dollar tip to watch my car...and my stuff...*especially my stuff.*

Instead, he stole everything I owned in the world...the car...the clothes...all gone. I didn't have money for food, so I fasted for a week while I stayed at the YMCA. When I ran out of money, I went to the Salvation Army. It was rough—especially since the next morning was Christmas. I walked to church in the snow. I only had $3.25 left when I went to a diner and ordered bacon and eggs. As I was reading my Bible the Scripture jumped out at me: "No eye has seen, no ear has heard, no mind has conceived what God has prepared for those who love Him, but God has revealed it to us by His Spirit" (1 Cor. 2:9-10, NIV).

I needed that Word. No, my circumstances did not change that day. But within one week eight miracles happened.

Yes! *Help was on the way.* I needed to just *get my flesh out of the way* so God could show up—*big time.*

David needed help all the time, and God sent him help. God wants to do the same for you, too.

David returned home to Ziklag one day to find out that he had lost everything. All his children and wives—everything was gone, taken by the Amalekites. His men were so angry that they wanted to stone David. But David knew that help was on the way, and he "strengthened himself in the Lord his God" (1 Sam. 30:6, NKJV).

David prayed, David worshiped, and he called on his priest Abiathar for counsel. He marched six hundred of his men fifteen miles to the brook Besor. Two hundred of the men stopped there because they were exhausted. The remaining four hundred joined him to hunt the Amalekites who had done this.

David related that he had found a half-dead Egyptian on the side of the road and had compassion on him, giving him food and water. The Egyptian had been left to die by the Amalekites, but David saved his life. *The Egyptian knew where the enemy was and because of David's kindness gave David this invaluable information.* David's men regained everything that the Amalekites had taken, and more.

The Prayer of David is called a *"warrior's psalm"* to be prayed before going into battle—a prayer for victory in battle!

What battles do you need victory in? God is ready!

"David became greater [Hebrew = "a long stride"] and greater [Hebrew = "a large embrace"] for the Lord God of hosts was with him" (2 Sam. 5:10, NASB).

When David prayed this prayer with all of his heart, he became:

- God-defined

- God-embraced

- God-saturated

I was scrubbing the pots with sand; it was my turn to do the dishes. In the desert you use sand, not water. Water is too precious to waste.

Everyone else was already asleep. Jamie Buckingham had given the devotion at dinner about the "church in the Sinai in the Old Testament." I had the mother of all headaches. Earlier that day we had been planning to climb Mt. Sinai, where Aaron had held Moses' hands up for victory in battle (see Ex. 17:12).

I decided I didn't want to spend hours going "slowly 'round the mountain," so I took off my shirt and extra gear and ran straight up. By the time the team arrived, I had heatstroke and was sick as a dog. Bill, an astronaut from Florida, was giving a devotion on being one in Christ. I badly wanted to get off the mountain. I tried to pretend I was fine until I knew I could not stand it any longer.

"Bill," I said, "I'm sick, dehydrated, and have sunstroke." He gave me water and a shirt and hat and helped me down the mountain. I was very embarrassed. As I thought about the day, I kept thinking what a stupid idea it had been to come on this trip.

"How can I get out of this desert of snakes and scorpions?" I asked myself.

Wind and heat! It was awful. As I was complaining to the Lord, I picked up my Bible and opened it to where it told about the children of Israel and their murmuring and complaining (see Exodus chapter 16). The Lord asked me what was wrong. I admitted to the Lord that I was proud, stubborn, and rebellious. In addition, I didn't like to submit to authority! With that confession and admission of guilt, the Lord instantly forgave me, and my headache and fever left!

The next day we came up on a Bedouin tent. A panicky Arab woman heard that a doctor was in our team. Angus Sergeant was an internist. The woman brought her baby, who had an infection covering its entire head. The baby's head was matted with flies and green matter about one-half-inch thick. They had taken knives and burnt the baby's head, scarring her face, in trying to kill the infection. I thought Angus was our hope for the hour.

"I can't help. The infection has to come off. She needs surgery," Angus said. Suddenly I felt the compassion of our Lord for this little six-year-old girl. So I placed my big hand on the abscess and prayed in Hebrew.

I knew that the mother would understand some of the prayer because Hebrew and Arabic are very similar. Gib Jones, a professional photographer, took a picture. There was no sign of a change when we left.

The next morning Dr. Sergeant said, "I've got to operate on the little girl. I will do the best I can—otherwise she may not live." Angus was the first one in the tent. I waited outside. Three or four minutes passed, and then I heard him crying. I opened the flap. He held a dirty cup of tea in his hand. It was the best offering the poor Bedouin could give. He was crying as he lifted it up, saying, "Lord, this is the greatest physical miracle I have ever seen." The child was totally healed. "Nothing is left on her head and all the scars are gone. If you can heal this child you can keep me from what is in this cup." He swallowed it, rejoicing. I wept with him, blessing the Lord for allowing me to be a living sanctuary in the Sinai.

Yes. *Help was on the way! I* was the only thing hindering help's arrival. When I got out of the way Christ reached through me, and with a blast of glory healed that little girl.

There were times during David's desert experience that his life, like mine, must have seemed like an emotional roller coaster. Without Jehovah becoming his light, and enlarging his darkness, David would never have fulfilled his heavenly assignment.

Late one evening on our trek up Mount Sinai, everyone began to stumble as darkness descended. "Turn off your lights," Jamie said. "Let the light of the stars guide you. Your eyes will adjust." We did, and panic hit me for a moment. Like David, I was out of my comfort zone. I wanted to trust in myself, but my eyes needed to adjust to the darkness. Within moments, millions of stars were glowing like fire-flies…illuminating our path. How like we humans to try to create our own light…to focus on ourselves…rather than on "The Lord…my **light** and my salvation…" (Ps. 27:1, KJV).

Chapter 4

GOD NEVER FORGETS

❧

"May He remember all your gifts and look favorably upon your burnt offerings."

David began his ministry celebrating an offering that Samuel had presented to God in Bethlehem. He did not know then that the greatest offering ever known would be given to the world in Bethlehem...the Lamb of God...pure and spotless.

Does God really want me to pray in faith, and anticipate His response to my gifts and offerings to Him? *Yes! A thousand times yes!*

Giving, for David, was an *act of worth-ship* ascribing worth to the Lord.

Why would God want you to know that giving a tithe and an offering to God is a holy act of *worth-ship* that commands a blessing on the giver? Because **when we give we are taking on the nature of God.** God is an extravagant giver. He not only gave us the greatest gift Heaven could afford—our Lord—but He also blessed the socks off of those in the Bible who trusted Him. Giving is an act of love and obedience and faith in God, virtues that the prince of this world does not have.

Before war, kings presented sacrifices (offerings), the acceptance of which determined their success.

David needed to know that God would remember his offering. *He needed victory in the battle.* David felt unworthy, but he knew his feelings were not the determining factor for victory—it was his mighty God's response.

God challenges us to prove Him. What a challenge—as if God needs to prove anything to us, but He does. Amazing!

"Bring the whole tithe into the storehouse, that there may be food in my house. Test me in this, says the Lord Almighty, and see if I will not throw open the floodgates of heaven and pour out so much blessing that you will not have room enough for it" (Mal. 3:10, NIV).

"Holy cow!" I shouted. "It's a miracle."

Cattle trucks were all over the place, and out came thirty head of cattle. David Wilkerson had recently dedicated our training center. We had led so many young people to Christ out of the drug culture that we felt they needed a place to be discipled. Now we would have all the beef we could eat—thirty head of Black

Angus cattle. David's prayer of dedication had included a word from the Lord that I pray will bless you.

The Sunday after the dedication, after praying according to the revelation of David's prayer in the Bible, I had given an offering of five hundred dollars to my church. I wrote on the check "Holy Cows"...and there they were!

Excitedly, I called Ben Martin, the vice president of my board.

"Ben," I shouted. "Holy cow! It's a miracle. God has given us twenty-nine bulls and a cow!"

"What?" Ben asked.

"God has given us twenty-nine bulls and a cow...or is it twenty-nine cows and a bull?"

"Mike," said Ben, "twenty-nine bulls and a cow wouldn't be much of a miracle. Are you sure it's not twenty-nine cows and a bull? Now THAT would truly be a miracle. You'd better go look again."

This city slicker knew nothing about the anatomy of cattle! I had no earthly idea whether God had provided one cow or twenty-nine! But I did know that God had miraculously answered my prayer!

Well, I looked, and sure enough, Ben was right! God had provided twenty-nine cows and a bull...the means for the ministry to start its own herd of Black Angus cattle. What excited me most is that the Scripture says, "Give, and it shall be given unto you...pressed down, and shaken together, and running over" (Lk. 6:38, KJV).

David prayed that Jehovah would remember our offerings.

- Burnt offerings were holy offerings.

- They cost something.

- They were a true sacrifice.

Christ was indeed the greatest burnt offering ever given to us from the Father.

An offering that really costs us something, not an offering of convenience but an offering that really challenges our faith, is a burnt offering. It's not like an offering that we know will not inconvenience us. It's a faith offering because we have to step out in faith to give it. Sometimes that offering requires us to put our flesh on the altar.

In 1972, I was in Texarkana, on the border between Texas and Arkansas. An old lady was carrying her heavy suitcase into the Holiday Inn.

"Excuse me. May I help you with your bag?" I asked as I ran up to her.

"Thank you," she said with a smile.

As I looked into her face, I was shocked to recognize Corrie ten Boom.

"I'm so honored to meet you. I read your book *The Hiding Place*," I told her.

"I would be honored if you would have a cup of soup with me," she responded sweetly.

"Yes, I'd love to," I said.

Corrie ten Boom shared with me her great love for God's chosen people and the prayers her family had prayed for them in their clock shop.

She shared her personal time of terror in prison, and how through a clerical error she had been released! She would have died in that prison had that "error" not occurred.

"Who is your favorite Bible figure?" I asked Corrie.

Without hesitation she said, "David. And one of my most favorite psalms is the ninety-first. I prayed it in prision, in Ravensbruk."

Corrie told me sitting there, "The secret place from the Ninety-first Psalm meant living before an audience of One. Christ's affirmation only comes when we pray. Otherwise we waste our lives seeking man! The entrance into the presence of God is through prayer. 'You shall find Me when you seek Me with all of your heart,'" she reminded me (Jer. 29:13, NIV).

Corrie began her ministry at fifty-two years of age—when most of us begin to think about "retiring."

Corrie had nothing—yet she had everything. She touched millions of people with the message of God's love. Corrie lived to be ninety-one.

As I am writing this it just hit me: I thought I would be dead by the age of twenty. Instead the Lord gave me a new name, Michael David, and a mighty word on which to stand—Psalms 20.

He turned my scars into a star! I have indeed found victory in my times of terror, even as Corrie had. And so can you.

Years later, I went to Holland to visit the "clock shop" where Corrie had saved many Jewish lives in the "hiding place." The owner had the door to the upstairs locked, and said it was only for storage.

"Lord, I want to buy this house and restore it so it can be a witness of Your love. Help me," I said prayerfully to God. The next day I asked the owner if he would sell the shop. He said "No," but as he said it all the clocks started chiming. It was noon. He looked at me and asked, "Do you know what day this is?" I replied that I didn't.

"Well, it is Corrie's birthday. And, yes, I will sell it to you."

For the last seventeen years, we have had the ten Boom home open, free of charge, as thousands have come…many weeping…while remembering the ten Boom family. Most of the family gave their lives to save Jewish people, to help them escape Hitler's hell and return to Palestine.

In Hebrew, *to remember* is "to recall," and *your gifts are presents! If you think of your offering as a present to God, it makes it very special.* Everyone loves a present.

Think on it—God is going to look favorably on the presents that you are giving Him.

We gave some gifts to friends yesterday. Dave said, "Mike, I'm embarrassed. I didn't know that we were exchanging gifts."

"We're not, Dave!" I said. "You will never give a gift to God without Him giving a better one back to you. He loves to give presents."

Many rabbis have told me that when God looks favorably on your offering, it also means that the offering may be "fat or fruitful," that your offering may produce abundant fruit in your life.

When God says *He will remember*, it means more than recalling something. *It's memorializing your offering or present!*

Offering was the basis in the Old Testament for answered prayer. Our Lord's offering became the basis of answered prayer for the world—a spotless Lamb

We are admonished to present our bodies as an offering to God.

And so, dear brothers, I plead with you to give your bodies to God. Let them be a sacrifice—holy—the kind He can accept. When you think of what He has done for you, is this too much to ask? "*Don't copy the behavior and customs of the world. But be a new and different kind of person with a fresh newness in all you do and think. Then you will learn from your own experience how His ways will really satisfy you*" (Rom. 12:2, LB).

When we make Jesus *Lord of everything,* it is only then that we can be sure we have been with Jesus.

We can expect a miracle when we give, because we are not our own anymore; we have surrendered all to Christ.

Prayer alone does not mean you've been with Jesus. Muslims pray; Hindus pray; murderers pray; rapists pray; and, as sick as it is, those who used our planes to kill thousands of Americans prayed—even on the planes. But praying God's word does mean you've been with Jesus. *You cannot pray the Word for an extended period of time and live in sin.*

We need to become so hungry and thirsty for Jesus that the mouth of hell is closed and the windows of Heaven are opened. May the lion of the tribe of Judah roar through us! May God give us a fresh revelation of the Father in the light of eternity!

There is no giver greater than God. He has *out-given* us all. He wants us to celebrate our giving and make it an act of *worth-ship*. He wants us to plant our seeds and expect a miracle harvest.

Why? Because the more we are blessed, the more we can be a blessing, as long as our hearts are pure.

A seed is a container of life. As long as this container remains alone, it cannot grow. Some seeds sit for decades with no growth and seemingly no purpose, until something breaks open the outer shell so the seed can interact with the soil and water to grow. A seed can sit for a hundred years in its own identity and accomplish nothing.

But when a seed becomes a burnt offering and dies, one seed can feed millions. Jesus is the best example of a seed dying and doing that.

A woman came to Jesus with a costly box of perfume, or "nard," worth an entire year's wages. She broke that box directly over Christ's head so that he would catch every drop of oil. The disciples grumbled that she had wasted money. But Christ was so moved, He said that she had anointed Him for His death and that wherever His gospel was preached the story of her offering would be told. (See John 12:3-7.) God remembers our gifts.

The box itself wasn't the fragrant offering for Jesus. The woman didn't paint or polish the box. She didn't try to get the box to smell like the perfume inside. Instead, she smashed the box so the purity of the nard inside could be released.

For the life of God to be released, God Himself, through Jesus Christ, had to go into the earth to die. We follow Christ's pattern. The person's outer shell—the natural man, not the body—has to die for the inner man to be released. *As long as we try to preserve the outer shell, keeping the flesh intact, the inner man will never be released. As long as we are enamored of our outer shell, we will never see the ministry of Jesus Christ live through us.*

"But we have this treasure in earthen vessels, that the excellence of the power may be of God and not of us" (2 Cor. 4:7, NKJV). We have to remember that the power is from God and is inside the jar, not outside. God literally placed the person of Jesus through the Holy Spirit in our earthen vessel! Only when our external fleshly part is broken can the power of the aroma of the treasure be received into Heaven.

One day, fully surrendered to the purposes of God, will render more fruit than a lifetime of good intentions.

When *religion* takes the place of Jesus, the life of Christ is *imprisoned* within believers, rather than *impassioned*.

David had an open heart, and an open heart proceeds and opens Heaven!

The present-day ministry of Jesus Christ operating through your life and mine will bring about a "God visitation" to transform a lost and dying world. This mighty move is going to be so big that people will start seeing the church house as a birth house because of the phenomenal number of new births. Staffed by ordinary Christians, it will be a Holy Spirit baby factory.

The only thing the members of the early church had with which to shake the world was that they had been with Jesus.

They sang the Twentieth through the Twenty-fourth Psalms in the book of Acts in their services.

- The Twentieth Psalm is a prayer.
- The Twenty-first is a praise.

- The Twenty-second is a prophecy.

- The Twenty-third is a present.

- The Twenty-fourth is a proclamation.

Why did the early church use the Twentieth through the Twenty-fourth Psalms in their worship? Because *"revelation determines reality!"* What God reveals to you is reality! King David said what God said! The words he spoke are the words of God— divinely inspired. He was saying what God says. He was praying what God says. You will be too, when you pray the prayers from these psalms.

Chapter 5

A KING IN TRAINING

"May he grant your heart's desire…"

My heart's desire was to get as far away from my father as possible. The United States Army beckoned, and I ran. "How far can you send me?" I asked the recruiting officer. "Korea," was his reply. And that's where I ended up…on a mountain called Wong Tong Nee. I was 17 years old, terrified and alone.

My first morning there, God gave me Psalms 5:2-3: "Hearken unto the voice of my cry, my King, and my God: for unto thee will I pray. My voice shalt thou hear in the morning, O Lord; in the morning will I direct my prayer unto thee, and will look up" (KJV). On top of that mountain in Korea, I gathered six big boulders and made a place of prayer. Every morning for fourteen months I prayed on that spot.

Almost twenty years later, I was invited to preach for Dr. Cho. He looked startled when I told him about my prayer place on Wong Tong Nee, and how shocked I was to discover, upon my return to South Korea, that the site was now Dr. Cho's Prayer Mountain. Literally thousands of people pray there daily. A million and a half people go there every year to pray! It was there that I had prayed in 1964 and 1965. Dr. Cho bought it in 1966! I was the first person to pray on Prayer Mountain. I had thought I was running away, but instead I ran right into the loving arms of my Savior. I learned, like David, that sometimes Gods stills the storms; other times, He stills us in the midst of the storm (see Ps. 107:29).

I went to Korea in a storm of fear and frustration. It was there that I learned that when you allow what God says to be the final word, you are stilled in the midst of your storm, even if the storm is still raging around you. I realized that God always provides a promise bigger than the problem...and defeats the demons of darkness. When we put what God says above our circumstances, our faith in His Word becomes the "fragrance of Heaven" that turns the head of God!

One promise from God, alive in your heart and your mouth, will provide provision in the midst of your predicament.

From the Sheepfold to the Slaughter Pen

Just as I was sent to Korea in the midst of international turmoil, so David was sent to Shochoh. His assigned task was to deliver food to his brothers in the midst of a battle with the Philistines. (See First Samuel chapter 17.)

As David approached the battlefield, he found himself in a battle...not between two armies, but between two men—Saul and Goliath. Saul was bowing; Goliath was bragging. Saul was cowering; Goliath was cursing. Saul was praying; Goliath was primping.

Terror was the order of the day! Goliath was a descendant of the Anakim, the same giants who had struck fear into the hearts of the spies Moses had sent into Canaan some four hundred years before. The rebellion in the ranks of the rescued had caused the children of Israel to wander in the desert for another forty years before they were allowed to enter the Promised Land.

Rebellion and discontent had again placed them in a valley of decision. Unhappy with God's plan, Israel demanded to be ruled by a king—Saul—rather than the King of kings.

Israel wanted to follow a proud king who refused to bend or bow and could not be broken. To their great regret, they received one in Saul. But God wanted the worship of a broken king who would gladly humble himself.

Although Saul stood head and shoulders above the men of Israel, he was no match for the real giant, fear.

Like his ancestors before him, Saul felt like a grasshopper in the presence of Goliath. Leaders today are often selected by the same criteria by which Saul was chosen...a good head for business, broad shoulders to bear the burden of business, impressive good looks. David was chosen because he was a man who longed to know the heart of God.

It seemed that Saul should have been the one to go into battle. The entire nation was trusting in the arm of flesh. After all, Saul looked like a king. He was trained. He had the armor. He was from the tribe of Benjamin, those experts with the slingshot! But a rock in the trembling hand of a fearful king would never find its mark. It would take pure uncompromising faith in an awesome God.

Religious flesh often disguises itself in kingly robes that hide the profane, ungodly heart. Jesus bluntly charged the scribes and Pharisees: *"Woe to you, teachers of the law and Pharisees, you hypocrites! You are like whitewashed tombs, which look beautiful on the outside but on the inside are full of **dead men's bones** and everything unclean"* (Mt. 23:27, NIV). When the world does not see, and say, "they have been with Jesus," our lack of faith and trust is evident. The works of the flesh...pride, lust, envy, hatred...manifest themselves...as opposed to the Fruit of the Spirit. Saul robed himself in religious flesh, wrapped himself in man-made armor, and trembled inside his tent. Saul said "No" to God, annulled his anointing, and relinquished his authority.

Then David arrived on the scene...a young shepherd from the hills of Bethlehem...a man so insignificant that

Saul didn't even remember that David had played the harp for him just months before. And miracle of miracles, David was not afraid of the strutting, self-centered Goliath! The future king in shepherd's garb stepped forward…unafraid, because he had been with God.

David knew that the key to the battle was allowing the Lord God Almighty to fight for him. He knew that success lay not in Saul's much-too-big armor, but in the full armor of God.

Most Christians today do not put on the armor of God. They choose, instead, Saul's religious armor. Thus, the battles of life consume them because they fight in their own strength. Too often, they think they have won the battle, only to find that they have lost the war! They are defeated by their own words and actions. Sadly, the casualties are their children, their marriages, and their ministries.

The weapons of David's warfare were not physical, but were "mighty through God to the pulling down of strong holds" (2 Cor. 10:4, KJV). When he fought Goliath, the miracle was not so much that a stone could kill a giant, even though he had on earthly armor; it was that David knew that he knew that he knew that the battle was the Lord's.

David had experienced the powerful presence of God while tending his father's sheep. He knew that the key to success was his relationship with Jehovah. David was fearless in the face of his enemy, because he had been on his face in the presence of the real King of Israel.

When Goliath tossed out his challenge—"Am I a dog, that thou comest to me with staves?…Come to me, and I will give thy flesh to the fowls of the air, and to the beasts of the field" (1 Sam. 17:43,44, KJV)—it simply bounced off David's helmet of salvation and breastplate of righteousness. David had already won the battle in his mind as he replied, "This day will the Lord deliver thee into mine hand...that all the earth may know that there is a God in Israel" (1 Sam. 17:45,46, KJV).

David's greatest battle turned into his greatest blessing. He was able to accomplish more in one hour with God than the entire nation was able to accomplish without Him. David chose to believe the words of God over those of his brothers, Saul, and the giant. When he made the decision to believe God, David made a God-connection. Only when you believe God, and therefore step out in faith, will you release God's power...and bring about a life-change.

David's determination to "follow his favor" led him from the sheepfold to the slaughter pen, from a cave to a palace. God's favor in my own life has led me from an abusive home to a mountain of prayer, from a dark depression to the halls of presidents and prime ministers. A friend and pastor used to say, "Mike, you have favor; follow it. Some people teach prophecy; you live it."

From Cave to Cave

David the hero, David the king's son-in-law, was running for his life! David had defeated Goliath, the giant Philistine. His second Goliath—Saul—was much more difficult to defeat. Do you have a Saul in your life…someone who bugs you, bothers you, and then bombs you?

The future king was now the hunted outlaw with a price on his head. Day and night for years Saul dogged David, just waiting for the moment when David would become vulnerable. The desire of Saul's heart was to plunge his spear through David.

Jealousy turns giants into jerks! Saul had a golden opportunity to demonstrate greatness when the Israelites sang, *"Saul has slain his thousands, and David his ten thousands"* (1 Sam. 18:7, NKJV). Saul could have taken a bow for sending David into battle. He could have become bigger in the eyes of the people. Instead, he became bitter.

Your success sometimes causes people to turn on you with a jealous rage. When that happens, know this: What God has told you in secret will keep you from giving up in the greatest battles of your life. Get your eyes off what you're going through…and get them on what you are going to!

Wet with sweat, alone, betrayed and weary, David took refuge in the cave of Adullam. *"And every one that was in distress, and every one that was in debt, and every one that was discontented, gathered themselves unto him; and he became a captain over them: and there were with him about four hundred men"* (1 Sam. 22:2, KJV).

There was no self-promotion for David. He was alone and cold in his cave. Things were going from bad to worse, but David refused to become a victim of "cave mentality." He was surrounded by the distressed (those under pressure or stress), by those in debt (people who could not pay their bills), and by the discontent (those bitter of soul). Did he fall into self-pity? Not David! He gathered those men around him and taught them how to become mighty men of valor!

Have you ever found yourself in a pit of despair—distressed, in debt, and discontented—hoping against hope that no one would come around? Step out of the darkness into the brilliant light of God's word!

It was not God's will for David to cave in to the pressure of the chase! David was destined for the throne. He was in the cave, but the cave was not in him! David was content to wait on God to elevate him to the place of honor. So David, the anointed shepherd-king and giant-killer, assumed the mantle of teacher and began to train his troops.

"The Lord is my light and my salvation; whom shall I fear? The Lord is the strength of my life; of whom shall I be afraid?" (Ps. 27:1, KJV)

"But ye are a chosen generation, a royal priesthood, an holy nation, a peculiar people; that ye should show forth the praises of him who hath called you out of darkness into his marvelous light" (1 Pet. 2:9).

Contentment is not the fulfillment of what you want, but the realization of how much you already have. Once you see that clearly through Christ and His Word, you will see a God bigger than your terrors.

Divine Appointment...Divine Deliverance

What a scene! What incredible odds! Saul and his three thousand special forces are pursuing David and his four hundred mighty men (see 1 Sam. 22:1). Saul is focused on only one thing—killing David!

David, the fugitive, and his rag-tag band flee to the wilderness of Judea. They take refuge at Ein Gedi— which literally means "spring of the goat."

After eleven days of trekking across the Sinai...following in the footsteps of Moses...I jumped for joy at the sight of the spring of Ein Gedi. Actually, I jumped with joy *into* the spring of Ein Gedi. It was my first bath in two weeks, and I was filthy!

Our band of eleven, which included the former astronaut, now congressman, Bill Nelson, and the great Christian author who is now in Heaven, Jamie Buckingham, stood in awe as we gazed at the towering walls of Ein Gedi. It would have been the perfect place for David to hide from Saul.

David had an appointment with Deity, but he first had to pass the test of divine confrontation!

> *"After Saul returned from pursuing the Philistines, he was told, 'David is in the Desert of En Gedi.' So Saul took three thousand chosen men from all Israel and set out to look for David and his men near the Crags of the Wild Goats. He came to the sheep pens along the way; a cave was there, and Saul went in to relieve himself. David and his men were far back in the cave. The men said, 'This is the day the Lord spoke of when he said to you, "I will give your enemy into your hands for you to deal with as you wish."' Then David crept up unnoticed and cut off a corner of Saul's robe"* (1 Sam. 24:1-4, NIV).

Saul was delighted with the news that David had been sighted. Finally, his rival would die like a dog in the desert. But God had another plan for both David and Saul.

Needing a quiet place to refresh himself, Saul entered one of the many caves in the area...not knowing that David and a handful of his men were hidden far back in the cave. Picture the scene: Saul was crouching in the privacy of the cave. He was totally vulnerable. Suddenly the kingdom was within David's grasp. A quick thrust of a spear and David would be king! His men whispered, "Do it! Kill him! He's evil; you're the chosen and anointed one. This is your moment of destiny."

David had been associate pastor of this flock for years. The path to the palace had been hard and rocky. Danger and death had been his constant companions. His congregation was full of moaners and complainers. Maybe God wanted the senior pastor out, even if it meant stabbing him in the back. Maybe David was the one to do it. After all, he was next in line to the pulpit.

Perhaps you know something about a coworker that, if revealed, would put you directly in line for that big promotion. Do you take the shortcut, the broad way...or do you stick to the narrow path of divine direction?

David's vision was within his reach. One swift thrust, and he was out of the pit and into the palace. Yet he knew that that vision would have to stay on the altar of sacrifice. David knew that "*except the Lord build the house, they labor in vain that build it*" (Ps. 127:1, KJV). He knew that there are no shortcuts to the throne. Even religious flesh filled with sound reasoning cannot take you to the fulfillment of your vision. David may have been at rock bottom, but he was determined to stand on the Rock and not compromise.

David's spirit was still strong. *"The Lord is my light and my salvation; whom shall I fear? The Lord is the strength of my life; of whom shall I be afraid?"* (Ps. 27:1, KJV)

"I waited patiently for the Lord; and he inclined unto me, and heard my cry. He brought me up also out of an horrible pit, out of the miry clay, and set my feet upon a rock, and established my goings" (Ps. 40:1-2, KJV).

The integrity of David's heart...the very character that caused God to choose him...prevailed. David persuaded him men to spare Saul. *"He said to his men, 'The Lord forbid that I should do such a thing to my master, the Lord's anointed, or lift my hand against him; for he is the anointed of the Lord'"* (1 Sam. 24:6, NIV). Instead of murdering him, David slipped silently forward in the cave and sliced off the edge of Saul's robe.

When we take personal vengeance into our own hands, it is at great cost to our souls. Let God be God...He will vindicate. *"'Vengeance is mine, I will repay,' saith the Lord"* (Rom. 12:19, KJV).

It has been said that the true test of character is what we do when we think no one is looking. David has passed the test. He knew that what he received in fulfillment of his desires in public would be measured by his devotion to the King in private. David embraced the promise, and God provided power in the midst of his predicament.

The Holy Spirit of God moved David to create Psalms 34 and 56 at Adullam and Psalms 31 and 54 at Ein Gedi. From the depths of despair, David wrote:

"*I will bless the Lord at all times; his praise shall continually be in my mouth*" (Ps. 34:1, KJV).

"*What time I am afraid, I will trust in thee*" (Ps. 56:3, KJV).

"*In thee, O Lord, do I put my trust; let me never be ashamed: deliver me in thy righteousness*" (Ps. 31:1, KJV).

"*Behold, God is mine helper, the Lord is with them that uphold my soul*" (Ps. 54:4, KJV).

David embraced God's word; Saul rejected God's word. David put God first; Saul put himself first. David fell on his face before the angel of the Lord (see 1 Chron. 21:16); Saul fell on his sword and committed suicide (see 1 Sam. 31:4). David lifted his hands to present an offering (see 2 Sam. 6:17); Saul hid that which God told him to destroy (see 1 Sam. 15:9).

Saul's enemy wasn't David. Saul's greatest enemy was Saul, and his own fleshly pride. Saul's battle was not against the Philistines; it was against God's spirit. There was no possibility that Saul could win in the spirit what he had already lost in the flesh. Saul lost his inheritance by placing his kingship first—rather than the King. Saul's choice cost him not only his inheritance; it cost him everything.

David's passion in life was to dwell in the presence of the Lord, to provide a dwelling place in his heart and in Jerusalem. This seed was planted as a young shepherd boy, watered by Samuel's anointing, and matured by Saul's pursuit and God's deliverance. David developed a heart attitude that moved God to action.

David was willing to place his faith in the King and pay whatever price was necessary.

Chapter 6

GOD WILL MOVE HEAVEN AND EARTH FOR YOU

❧

"...and fulfill all your plans!"

David the shepherd-king wanted to establish a kingdom for the King of kings! He had so many heart's desires and plans. He also had many enemies who desired only to see him fail.

One of David's biggest enemies was David. God had to exhaust David many times in order to fulfill David's heart's desire and plans. It was always going to be on God's timetable—not David's.

What are your desires and plans?

David was on a slow train to Jerusalem. Years had gone by since his anointing, and it looked like it just wasn't going to happen. Well, it did, but it happened on **God's** timetable, not David's.

Does it sound familiar?

Imagine God asking you to give everything you owned—including your name—to someone else who would do more with it than you would. Imagine giving:

- Your talent

- Your career

- Your family

- Your possessions

- Your reputation

- Everything you've ever been

- Plus everything you could potentially become, to another person, in hopes that they would accomplish more than you would.

That's exactly what Jesus did.

Jesus let go of everything He had—His power, His reputation, His name, His life, His history, His words, His very spirit, everything He'd ever been and everything He ever would be—and He gave it to us.

Then Christ departed physically to sit at the Father's right hand in Heaven. Why? Jesus knew, beyond any shadow of a doubt, that there would come a day when the people who were called by His name would fulfill all His prophecies and answer all of His prayers.

"Anyone who believes in me will do the same works I have done, and even greater works, because I am going to be with the Father" (Jn. 14:12, NLT). If Jesus is alive in us it's time for us to realize that Jesus has a present-day ministry in the now. He wants to establish His kingdom in us and reign on the throne of our lives. When that happens His heart's desires will be yours, His plans will be yours, and He will move heaven and earth if need be to accomplish them.

American troops were in the Persian Gulf; Saddam Hussein had invaded Kuwait.

I had just had major surgery on my neck—eight hours under the knife. I was sick, and couldn't take the pain medicine because it made me sicker, and I was depressed. Satan was saying to me, "You are toast! It's over. You'll never recover from this." I prayed, "Lord, You said You would give me my heart's desire and fulfill my plans. I thank You that today You are healing me."

Little did I know the power of that prayer! Instead of a physical miracle, the Lord said, "You said you wanted to do something great for me. Then do it! Go to Saudi Arabia and preach the gospel!"

"Lord," I said, "I can't go—they will cut my head off." Then I started to laugh. I was worried about my head.

"Oh well, they wouldn't have much to cut off," I thought.

"Apply for a visa to Saudi Arabia," the Lord said.

"Lord, I can't. They won't give me one."

"How do you know? You've never tried."

"Billy Graham doesn't even have one," I said.

"Yes, I know, but he never applied. Just do it," the Lord continued.

I obeyed the Lord's prompting—commanding, rather—got that visa, and was soon on my way to Dhahran, Saudi Arabia, with the back of my head shaved because of the surgery, and staple marks on the side and back of my neck.

I arrived very late at night and went to the Gulf Meridian Hotel. I knew no one.

God was going to have to move big-time because here I was—sick and not knowing what in the world to do. The next morning, I got on my knees and prayed, "Father, my heart's desire is to please You."

"What do I do now?" I asked Him after praying.

I heard the Lord say in my spirit, "Go to the Dhahran International Hotel and shake the hand of the first man you see going through the door. Say, 'May I go with you?'"

I went to the hotel. When the first man came through the door, I reached out, shook his hand and said, "May I go with you?"

"Who are you?" the man asked in shock.

"Mike Evans," I said.

"Where are you from?"

"Texas."

"How did you get here?"

"British Airlines. I know you may think I am a madman, but I'm not. I want to go with you."

"OK. You will go. Be here tomorrow at 6:15 a.m."

I arrived at 5:45 a.m. and waited in the dark lobby. At 6:15 a.m., Jeeps drove up to the hotel. In the fourth Jeep were the general in command of the Saudi Royal Air Force, the governor of Bahrain, and the commander of the Multinational Forces. The same man whose hand I had shaken, General Khaled bin Sultan, was going to the Kuwaiti border to meet with the commanders of the Egyptian Third Army and the Syrian High Command. General Khaled bin Sultan. On the trip I shared with him about Jesus Christ.

"The cross is making me nervous," he said. "You know, I think you're trying to convert me. We cut heads off for that. Would you like to go there on Thursday?"

"No thanks," I said, "I've got a busy day Thursday, and can't work it into my schedule." He laughed.

"I like you," he said.

"I'm glad," I said. "I'm a friend of Jesus, and look at my hands. God will give you your land back in fewer days than the fingers on my hands, and with the shedding of hardly any blood. Jesus says to tell you this," I spouted out.

"Oh, you must be a prophet. If this comes to pass we will invite you to Kuwait to speak to the royal family about Jesus and His cross."

I smiled. Yes, God. You are great!

On that trip, I shared Christ with Egyptians and with Syrian commanders. It was truly a divine appointment. The depression and the pain in my neck left. I totally forgot about the surgery. I was doing big business for my God. This was indeed a great plan. He did tell me, at eleven years old, that he had a great plan for my life.

When I got back, I went into the center of town and just started preaching. A military colonel came up to me.

"Are you nuts?" he said. "We are going to lock you up in jail to save your life before you get your head cut off."

I just smiled and said, "Come to my room. I would be honored to go to jail for Jesus. We'll have a Paul and Silas service."

That night as I got to the hotel, Kuwaiti sheiks with worry beads saw me and said, "You're a friend of Arafat." One of them remembered seeing me in 1988 at the United Nations General Assembly specially convened session.

I hadn't been invited to that session, but the Lord had told me to go.

"But, Lord, I am not invited!" I argued. "I am not a minister of a government."

"You're not?" the Lord asked. "You don't think My kingdom is a government? Just go, and I will open the door."

I went in obedience, and of course He did open doors. I found myself in the General Assembly for all the sessions. I shared Christ with forty-three foreign ministers, and I received a card from each one of them. It was an incredible experience.

In the evening, Arafat was speaking in a special press conference. Of course, I was not invited. That morning, the Lord told me to go to a room. He sent me to the first row of seats next to the table. He told me to put my briefcase there and lock it. As I left for my hotel, a man walked up to me outside of the General Assembly, spat on my shoe and said, "If you open your mouth against Chairman Arafat, I will blow your head off!"

The anointing of God was upon me that evening as I went back to the room where Arafat and his executive committee of terrorists were meeting. The door was locked and heavily guarded. The room was full of guests, all there by *invitation only. I realized that this was the room where God had told me to leave my briefcase.*

"Excuse me, sir," I said to the guard. "I need to go to my seat."

"What seat? You have no seat here," he said.

"Yes," I said. "Go to the front and open my briefcase. Its combination is 1001."

He did and came back and escorted me to my seat. Minutes later, Arafat came in. I was directly in front of him in the middle seat. After his speech, which was covered live by the world press, he told the group that they could choose three among us to ask a question.

I knew they would not choose me, so I spoke up.

"Mr. Arafat, Jerusalem is the Jewish capital of the State of Israel where the Jewish Messiah will return."

"Shut up, shut up! What must I do to make you shut up—striptease for you? It would be absurd," Arafat said in his pedantic English.

He screamed as I continued talking. *Fear hit me.*

"Lord," I said, "If you have sent me here to conquer my fear, it has not worked. They're going to kill me! You divided the sea for Moses. I only need a few feet to get out of this room."

Suddenly it was as if a carpet had been rolled out. I stepped out into the dark hallway. As I walked along, it seemed like forever before I found a way out.

"Have no fear—a cab will be waiting with the door open," the Lord said to me. "Get in and go to your hotel. The phone will be ringing. No man will hurt you."

Yes, the cab was there, and yes, when I arrived in my room at the Hilton Hotel in Geneva the phone was ringing. It was Reuben Hecht, the senior advisor to the prime minister of Israel.

"Mike, we are hearing you in Israel. How many bodyguards do you have? Arafat is a terrorist, and his people are also," Advisor Hecht said over the phone.

"Oh, I have many guards—they are angels."

"Good ones," Reuben responded.

"Yes, Reuben, real good ones." He didn't know that I meant heavenly angels.

"In that case, will you speak for Israel tomorrow after the ambassador speaks?"

"I would be honored," I told him.

Never again have I been afraid of a terrorist. God answered my prayer and delivered me from the fear of terror in a most amazing way.

Several days later my heavenly orders came to go to Iraq. I went and preached there also. My last sermon, held in a muddy field, was on Jonah and Nineveh. I spoke to several hundred people, but only one old man came forward to receive Christ. I was disappointed. I had hoped that at least thirty or forty would come forward. When I saw the man's tears and joy, I rejoiced with him.

My interpreter was bouncing with excitement. I couldn't understand. He kept saying, "Can you believe it? Can you believe it?"

"Believe what?" I asked.

"You don't know what happened, do you?"

"Yes I do. He found the Lord."

"No, I mean yes, but that's not what I'm so excited about. This sheik is Kurdish. He rules over sixteen provinces and his capital city of Nineveh. Yes, you just led the king of Nineveh to Christ. He has invited you to come to Nineveh and share Christ. They will repent also."

I was bone tired, but thrilled to see the plans of God, and I felt fulfilled.

"Lord, can I go home now?"

"No," He said. "Go to Jerusalem."

Iraq was attacking with SCUDs as I stood at the check-in desk of the Hyatt Regency Hotel in Jerusalem. The hotel was jammed. The Israelis from Tel Aviv and Haifa had come there, knowing that Saddam would not fire on Jerusalem. He feared that he would miss and blow up the Mosque of Omar. An old rabbi came up to me. He was short, and I bent down. In his hand, he was holding a gas mask in a cardboard box.

"Have you come for a tour? This is not a good time to go on tours," the rabbi said.

"No," I said, "I haven't come for tours."

"Why do you have smiling eyes? I see you're not afraid. You have peace; I can see it. Are you taking drugs?" he asked me.

"No, but I am taking a pill…a Gos-pill," I replied.

David realized that his plans and desires would never be fulfilled in his own strength, and neither will ours. *We cannot do things of eternal value without a red-hot prayer life.*

The eyes of God are searching for hungry hearts that are willing to surrender to the person of the Holy Spirit and thirst to be with Jesus. Christ has determined that we will rule and reign with Him. It's His mission, not just when we get to Heaven, but while we are on this earth.

There is a place in Christ that will quench all the fiery darts of the enemy, no matter what the circumstance. With self in charge, we meagerly try to contact God—flesh to Spirit. With Jesus on the throne of our lives as Lord and king, we experience spirit-to-spirit contact. While we fear God, we will never fear man. *When we have been with Jesus, we will never surrender that intimacy to dance to another man's song.* But if we spend all of our time trying to be man-pleasers, we will ride a merry-go-round of repentance and regret. Man-pleasing is spiritual fornication when Christ is trying to embrace His bride.

When we allow the King to rule unchallenged in our lives, our greatest passion is to see God do His work through us…anywhere…anytime…in any way.

Jesus has called you "into his kingdom and his glory" (1 Thess. 2:12, RSV). We have been called into Christ's kingdom on earth. The battle that Christ waged with satan wasn't over God's kingdom in Heaven. Heaven's kingdom was already firmly established and was not subject to satan or in conflict with satan. Christ defeated satan to establish the kingdom of God on this earth.

Fulfilling our destiny comes through experiencing God's power. But we cannot have His power without His presence. We enter into God's presence through prayer!

The King of Glory is raising up an army of mighty men and women who seek no temporal throne or temporal power, carry no carnal weapons of might, and do not stockpile the praises of men. Dead to themselves, their only hope is to be seated in heavenly places with

Christ, the hope of glory. They alone terrorize the demons of hell and torment principalities and powers, because they cannot be bought by ambition. They alone will usher in the greatest harvest the world has ever seen.

These soldiers of the King do not chase "super-stars" of the faith hoping to get their Bible auto-graphed. They see only One, Bright and Morning Star, Jesus, who has written His name on the tablets of their hearts. They lay their plans at His feet and embrace His plan for their lives. For them, the person of the Holy Spirit is no longer imprisoned by flesh on the throne. In their wombs the seed of God is coming alive to birth His destiny on the earth. They are not simply burden-bearers for the high and mighty; they are warriors, commissioned by the Lion of Judah to gather the nations before Him.

In the same way that intimacy between a husband and a wife produces life, intimacy between Jesus and His bride produces life.

David knew how to get into the presence of a holy God. He knew that was the key.

Jesus planned a magnificent destiny for you, and gave you incredible prayers and prophecies.

Have you been with Jesus?

Your family will know when you have. Your friends will know, and more importantly, the lost will know. When we've been with Jesus, a consuming fire burns in our bones. Idols are cast down. Anything that takes the place of Christ's lordship is gone.

Idols are destroyed because our pride is broken. The Bible says, "The sacrifice you want is a broken spirit. A broken and repentant heart, O God, you will not despise" (Ps. 51:17, NLT).

Have you been with Jesus? If you have, the Word is alive—burning in your bones.

Have you been with Jesus? If you have, you no longer fear man.

Have you been with Jesus? If you have, He has made known unto you the mystery of His will, which is His good pleasure.

Yes, God is ready to move heaven and earth for you if you have been with Jesus.

He is ready to fulfill all of your plans and your heart's desires.

Instead of Jesus only appearing in Bethlehem, because David made a God-connection, the King will appear in your spirit to fulfill His destiny through you!

Why not stop and pray the Prayer of David right now?

Prayerlessness is the bacterium that causes the disease of unbelief.

God moved heaven and earth for you at Calvary!

This revelation seems to have been held in reserve for a few chosen vessels. But those days are over…IT'S HARVEST TIME. Jesus is coming soon!

Chapter 7

TOMORROW'S NEWS TODAY!

*"May we shout for joy when we hear of your victory,
flying banners to our God!"*

Remember that this prayer is not really David's alone. Jehovah gave it to David under the inspiration of the Holy Spirit! It was divinely inspired, as is all Scripture. Yes, David was the first one to pray it! So we call it the Prayer of David.

Think of this passage—"Shout for joy...when we hear of your victory...flying banners to our God!"

It's a heavenly blank check signed by the Lord.

What a promise! David proclaims, by faith, that this prayer will be answered and what will happen when it is answered?

David was a *shouter.* He became the torchbearer of the revelation.

Jesus rejoices that He is from the seed of David! "I, Jesus, have sent my angels to testify to you these things in the church. I am the Root and the Offspring of David. The Bright and Morning Star" (Rev. 22:16, NKJV).

Amazing grace! David would not have even been a seed had it not been for "the Seed" Jesus.

Jesus is so worthy. He blesses and honors the seed that He creates. Warts and all.

Are we blessed or what?

Heaven rejoices over the salvation of one single soul. I'm sure it is with shouts of joy. David is telling us that there are going to be *shouts of joy* by more than one person (by all of us—you included if you so desire!) over the answer to this prayer.

There is a lot of shouting in the Bible. "The Lord...shall descend...with a shout!" (1 Thess. 4:16, KJV)

"Shout joyfully to the rock of our salvation" (Ps. 95:1, NASB).

"Make a joyful noise [shout] all ye lands" (Ps. 66:1, KJV).

Shouting for joy and victory was a form of *worthship.* The walls are coming down...SHOUT! Blow the trumpet and shout unto God.

Angels shout! Jesus shouts! The saints shout! GLORY!!! HALLELUJAH!!! BLESS THE LORD!!!

But we are promised a shout from Heaven when our prayer is answered!

At the young age of thirty-one, I had to check into a cardiology ward. I had been working eighteen-hour days, seven days a week, for years. That wasn't smart, and it certainly wasn't taking care of God's temple in me. It was stress that created my problems.

I hadn't had a heart attack! But the doctor said, "You had better slow down, or you will."

My depression got worse and worse, and I began having panic attacks. I even stopped preaching and walked away from our ministry in New York. I lost my joy, my shout of victory, and my hope.

For one year, I sat on the steps of our headquarters and cried in the dark.

I moved back to Texas, utterly defeated. At the same time, I was having major problems with my neck. I couldn't keep it from shaking. It really looked as though I were having a breakdown. After eight years, I was diagnosed with a rare neurological disease. My head not only shook; it also turned upward. All the muscles in my neck were in spasms. I was so very broken.

I even took a real estate course. My plan was to leave the ministry and God's calling on my life. (That was the problem—it was MY plan—not God's plan.)

A pastor kept asking me to preach for him. I didn't want to, but I finally told him I would.

"Lord, I have no joy, no peace. I don't know what else to do but quit," I cried, as I looked out the plane window. "I'm so ashamed."

The Lord spoke to me on that plane and gave me a Scripture. He told me to go to the room, pray it, and shout and shout and shout…not in anger but in faith.

So I stood on one Scripture, praying it over and over and shouting.

That Scripture was Isaiah 43:18-19.

"Do not remember the former things, nor consider the things of old. Behold I will do a new thing, now it shall spring fourth; shall you not know it? I will even make a road in the wilderness and rivers in the desert" (Is. 43:18-19, NKJV).

I posted it in my car, in my office, on the mirror, even on the trash can, so that every time I put something in the trash, I would see that Scripture. I made it into a card and put it in my wallet. I thought about it, prayed it, and meditated on it. Looking back, I can say with certainty that almost everything God has done in my life has come when I prayed, received a Scripture and a Word from God, and stood on it. Uncompromisingly! No matter what I felt, what the circumstances looked like, or what other people were telling me—I stood on that Word. It didn't even matter what I was telling myself—I made that Word the final authority in my life!

I realize now that when we make the Word the final authority in our life, we are making the Lord the final authority in our life. You can't believe the Word without surrendering to the lordship of Christ. Your faith explodes when you pray the Word with all of your heart!

When I arrived home I told my wife, Carolyn, that God had spoken to me through Isaiah 43:18-19.

"I am standing on this Word until hell freezes over," I said.

I had decided to go to Israel.

"Honey, why are you going to Israel?" Carolyn asked.

"To meet with Begin," I said.

"Do you have an invitation?" she asked.

"No, but God said 'Go,' and I know that He is sending me. I can't run any longer.

I can't win this battle, but God can. I will have to just roll all of my cares over on Him. He cares for me."

Yes, I went. I checked into the hotel and prayed for a week. I had sent a wire to Prime Minister Begin asking for a meeting. There truly was no way in the normal course of things that he would meet with me. Well, he did. For thirty minutes I said nothing while he talked about having a heart attack and other problems.

"Mike, why did you come?" he finally asked.

"I don't know why. I only know God sent me."

He smiled and said, "Shake my hand. I have finally met an honest man. You don't know why you came—all you know is that God sent you. I like that. Do me a favor when God tells you why—come back and tell me why. I'm very curious."

I left his office shouting, knowing that in the midst of my agony God was revealing my destiny. He did say He had a great plan for my life at the age of eleven.

Later I went back to Prime Minister Begin. I told him I knew why God had sent me.

"Build a bridge," I told him.

"A bridge," he laughed. "Like the Brooklyn Bridge?"

"No," I said. "A bridge of love between Christians and Jews in Israel."

"Great, I will help you build that bridge." He and I became dear friends, and met often.

Yes, I had had a time of terror in every way! But God had not left me for a moment.

He was only waiting for me to believe what He believes.

No, I have never looked back since that dark season. I only rejoice in the greatness of our God!

That first year I received 18,500 "thank you" letters from Jewish people for the work we were doing in building a bridge of love.

When God says, "Yes," you can take it to the bank. It will come to pass.

"What is faith? It is the confident assurance that what we hope for is going to happen" (Heb. 11:1, NLT).

"The battle is the Lord's" (1 Sam. 17:47, KJV).

Banners flying were a part of military equipage, borne in times of war to assemble, direct, distinguish, and encourage the troops. They were used also for celebrations. The banner was to acknowledge His glory and to implore His favor.

Deliverance is on the way. When the children of Israel left the Sinai to possess the Promised Land, they marched under banners.

A banner was an ensign. The banners that are flying for the believer today have the name of our God, Yeshua (Jesus), on them. Their color is red for the power of the blood; the streamer is for the word of the gospel—the good news.

May we shout for joy over you when we hear of your victory, flying banners over you, too!

Honor our God. What a promise! David remembered that his boast was in the name of His God. Rejoice that all the giants in his life and yours bend their knee to that mighty name.

"All those gathered here will know that it is not by sword or spear that the Lord saves: for the battle is the Lord's" (1 Sam. 17:47, NIV).

God rewrote the text of David's life by the power of His mighty hand, and He will do the same for you. You win because He has already won.

Chapter 8

A HEAVENLY GUARANTEE

∽

"May the Lord answer all your prayers."

What are your prayers? Do you dare to praise Him in faith, believing that He will answer all of your prayers?

David would not have prayed this prayer if it were not possible.

How many people do you know with glowing testimonies of answered prayer who were "doubt pushers"?

If God told David through the person of the Holy Spirit to pray "May the Lord answer all of your prayers," then I have a legal right to come boldly to the throne of grace.

Notice it says may the "Lord" answer all of your prayers. We have to make Him Lord to qualify for this wonderful blessing!

How do I make Christ Lord?

By putting Christ first in everything, every day! Jesus first. A lost and dying world is staring down the tunnel of eternity; only a people that have made Jesus Lord can rescue multitudes.

Dethrone self daily as you pray the Prayer of David. "Not my will, Lord, but may Yours be done in my life today."

God does not consult with me to determine His plan or purpose through me. It is my responsibility to consult with Him. I must be in His will; He has made no provision to be in my will. All our prayers can be answered as we understand this principle.

When self is on the throne of our lives, we can be sure that chaos will be the norm, no matter how religious or sincere we are. Chaos is a sure sign that we have not been with Jesus. Chaotic Christianity distorts the image of the living Savior. To be sure, a chaotic Christian will never know the abundant Christ-life. To them it will be only a myth.

How heartbreaking when we settle for tradition! The habit is formed, but the hunger is lost. Our hunger for God is the greatest indication of who is on the throne of our lives.

The flesh desires to conquer the cross, ignore it, and disregard Christ's lordship. The Cross desires to conquer the flesh and eradicate its lordship!

In the wombs of Christians, the Lord Jesus Christ abides through the person of the Holy Spirit because of the new birth. Most of us dropped everything when we caught a glimpse of His thumb, His toe, or maybe His ear, and went off to worship a small part of our Lord.

But those who desire to make Jesus Lord refuse to comfort themselves with past victories. They are not content with being Heaven-gazers like those in the book of Acts whom the angels rebuked (see Acts 1:11). When Jesus is Lord, we will be content with nothing except seeking His face until we see His face. "Face to face beholding his Glory."

God is listening for the heartbeat of Jesus in you. When the Father hears it, all Heaven will be authorized to move on your behalf.

Our generation has a divine appointment with destiny. What we do with Christ will echo throughout eternity.

We must confess that our secular society has retarded and repackaged our Christian values and filtered them back to the church, watered down, neutered, and left lifeless—leaving Christ-ianity in a state of passivity.

Lord, may you answer all my prayers! And may you be an answer to our Lord's prayer.

"Anyone who believes in me will do the same works I have done, and even greater works, because I am going to be with the Father" (Jn. 14:12, NLT).

God told me when I was eleven years old that He had a great plan for my life! I have always believed that.

When America announced that the U.S. and Russia were hosting the Madrid Peace Conference in 1991 following the Persian Gulf War, I knew that Jesus was going to be there. You cannot have a peace conference without the Prince of Peace in attendance…even though He didn't have an invitation.

I flew to Madrid believing that God would answer my prayer and set before me "an open door that no one can shut" (Rev. 3:8, NIV). As the cab driver drove off, he asked me where I was going. Since I really didn't know, I just said, "To the hotel where all the world leaders are staying."

"Oh, the Madrid Ritz," he replied.

"Yes," I said, "I guess everything begins tomorrow."

"No," he said, "the Israeli prime minister is meeting in the Russian Embassy now with the president of Russia, Gorbachev."

"Take me there, and hurry," I said.

He dropped me off in front of the gate and drove off. It was raining and cold. It was the wrong gate. I ran until I was winded to get to the other side of the Russian Embassy. The media from Russia were outside the gate yelling to get inside.

I joined them with a louder yell than those who were in charge. Russians like to be in charge. An embassy official came to the gate

"I am in charge," he said.

"I want to go inside," I told him.

"Where are your credentials?" he asked.

I had nothing except my Bible. I raised it and said, "Here are my credentials."

He looked at my Bible and turned to walk away.

"Sir, come here," I said.

He turned back, and I stuck my finger through the gate.

"In the name of Jesus Christ who has sent me here, open this gate and let me in." All of a sudden the gate opened, and in I walked in with tears streaming down my face.

God continued to give me favor, and I was in attendance at almost every session at the Royal Palace. At one break, the foreign ministers of Egypt and Syria asked me, "Are you a minister?"

"Yes. I am representing a kingdom."

"What kingdom?" they asked.

"The kingdom of God."

"We never heard of that one. It must be very small."

"Oh no, it's not. It's going to swallow up all of yours."

They laughed. "Are you Semitic?"

"Yes, I am."

I looked at the Egyptian foreign minister and said, "Why do you not obey the words of your most famous prime minister and secretary of state, who held both portfolios at the same time?"

"We never had such a man. If we did, I would most certainly honor his words."

I opened my Bible and read, "And Joseph forgave his brothers."

Yes indeed, God desires to answer all of your prayers!

It's time to declare war on Heaven-gazing! Gazers pollute the purposes of God. They saturate themselves with heavenly religious perfume, but live by their own agendas.

They short-circuit the power of God.

If Christ empowered gazers with "self" on the throne, it would make a mockery of the sacrifice He made at Calvary. The refusal to surrender complete control of our lives to Christ is a blatant declaration of war against His lordship.

Yes, God wants to answer our prayers, but self must get off the throne of our lives. When self is on the throne, the spirit of lawlessness infects and pollutes the house of God. Rather than damaging the gates of hell, precious pastors spend much of their time in damage control because of saints who refuse to relinquish the throne of their lives to the lordship of Christ. People want to use His name and have the fame.

It's time we rise up with holy indignation and determine that our lives will not be dumping grounds for satan's pollution.

Yes, God wants to answer our prayers. As we determine that we are going to live our lives in the light of eternity, answered prayer will be as normal as breathing.

You and I will never reign with Christ in the sunshine if we refuse to allow Christ to reign through us in the storms.

Our Lord meant it when He said "If you ask anything in my name I will do it" (Jn. 14:14, NKJV).

"If two of you agree on earth concerning anything that they ask, it will be done for them by My Father in heaven" (Mt. 18:19, NKJV).

We do have a Heavenly Guarantee.

This is the greater works generation.

God has proven time after time that He is the God of greater works, the God of the impossible, the God who opens doors.

"Honey, your friend has been killed," Carolyn said.

"Who?" I asked.

"Prime Minister Rabin," she said.

My heart was broken. I had prayed with him in Jerusalem and had written him a long letter. He was a great man.

"God, what do I do?" I prayed.

Israelis have funerals very quickly, and this was to be a state funeral. I didn't have an invitation.

"Go," the Lord said.

So I went. As the plane was landing, I couldn't believe my eyes. Representatives of all the nations of the world were there. Their planes were everywhere; there were more than 18,000 people in security details.

Queen Beatrice of the Netherlands, Prince Charles of England, Chancellor Helmut Kohl of Germany, Prime Minister John Majors, Presidents Jimmy Carter, Bill Clinton, and George H.W. Bush were there...eighty-six world leaders.

"You will not get within five miles of the state funeral," the cab driver said.

"You just drive, and I will pray."

"Can't I let you drive?" he asked. I laughed.

He was right. Miles from the funeral, the streets were blocked. The military was everywhere. I didn't have clearance for my cab, and neither did the driver. Normally, security forces would have turned us around very quickly.

Suddenly I heard a loud voice. "Get this cab out of here, now!"

I rolled down my window. The colonel looked at me and smiled. "Mike Evans, it's you. Oh well, you don't believe in 'No,' do you?"

"Not when God sent me, I don't."

"OK, go, but you'll never get through the security checkpoints."

We drove several miles on empty streets. I got out and went through two different checkpoints. No one said a word. As I was walking up the hill to the funeral, security guards were eyeing me, but no one spoke. I had no credentials except a pass from Heaven. As I stood a short distance from a world leader, I heard, "Mike Evans, put this pass on. How did you get in? Never mind. Don't tell anyone you got through all of our security. It would be a big embarrassment."

"Oh, Mike, did you not go to the Hyatt Regency Hotel? Your state invitation and pass are there."

"No, I came straight from the airport."

At the funeral, I held dozens of weeping Israelis in my arms, comforting them. Yes, God had sent me. He does answer all of our prayers when we are in His will.

Satan's greatest fear is the child of God who has been with Jesus, is completely yielded to the holy fire of the living God, and is fully manifesting the glory of God. Religion cannot deliver our families, our nation, our world, or even us. There is no time left to play the part. *There is only time to be the part.*

Child of God, you and I are staring into the face of an eternal countdown that cannot be stopped. It's time to seek the Lord. He is coming soon and the harvest is yet to be gathered.

"Arise, my people! Let your light shine for all the nations to see! For the glory of the Lord is streaming from you. Darkness as black as night shall cover all the peoples of the earth, but the glory of the Lord will shine from you. Nations will come to your light: mighty Kings will come to see the glory of the Lord upon you" (Is. 60:1-3, LB).

"The people that do know their God shall be strong and do exploits" (Dan. 11:32, KJV). Those who have insight will shine brightly like the brightness of the expanse of Heaven" (Dan. 12:3, NASB).

Our Lord began the New Testament with David, and ended it with David in the last chapter of Revelation. He read the same psalm you are reading! And I'm sure that He prayed it. The cross was a time of great terror! But thank God, because through His death and resurrection, you and I have been promised a new day!

Congratulations, it's your coronation day!

I told you that King David prayed this prayer and that it was used for coronations of kings!

When this prayer gets in your spirit…really in there…when you know that you know that you know, then get ready for your "coronation day"!

"What am I talking about," you ask? I'm talking about a God who anointed a shepherd to become one of his sheep, and in so doing, elevated that shepherd to the rights and privileges of kingship.

I'm talking about you. Yes, you! What God did for David, He wants to do for you.

"I'm no king," you say? Well, maybe you are and don't know it. Maybe you're just not thinking, walking, talking, and believing like one.

God says you are a king! Now what do you say about that?

You may be in a black hole like David was in every way, but do you now doubt that David was going to be a king?

If you don't like being a king, take it up with Jesus. He shed His blood so you could be His seed…and so you could inherit His last will and testament.

"To Him who loved us and freed us from our sins by His own blood and hath made us kings and priests to His God and Father, to Him be the glory and dominion forever and ever. Amen" (Rev. 1:5-6, RSV).

"Finally, there is laid up for me the crown of righteousness, which the Lord, the righteous Judge, will give to me on that Day, and not to me only, but also to all who have loved His appearing" (2 Tim. 4:8, NKJV).

Most Christians don't see themselves as kings under divine appointment. But Christ does. That is why He's so extravagant in His love toward you.

The more often you read this little book, the more you will become hungry for more of God!

The more you believe the Prayer of David and make it your own prayer, the more you will feel all Heaven break lose in your life when faith kicks in! *Get ready.*

You are a partaker of His divine nature through great and precious promises (see 2 Pet. 1:4).

You are qualified to be a partaker of the inheritance of the saints (see Col. 1:12).

"In Him also we have obtained an inheritance" (Eph. 1:11, NKJV).

David was given a military commission "to fight the fight of faith," and you have been, too.

A king kneels in a moment of solitude. The day of battle is about to begin. He is clad in full battle array. All the modern weapons of war are at his hand. He can hear the warriors' chants growing stronger. The burden of his responsibilities is so heavy. His advisors disagree with each other. There are traitors in the camp. Previous avenues of wisdom have dried up. Now the burden of decision is his alone. What is his next step?

Epilogue

THE WAY OF DAVID, THE KING

"For thou wilt save the afflicted people; but wilt bring down high looks. For thou wilt light my candle: the Lord my God will enlighten my darkness. For by thee I have run through a troop; and by my God have I leaped over a wall. As for God, his way is perfect: the word of the Lord is tried: he is a buckler to all those that trust in him. For who is God save the Lord? or who is a rock save our God? It is God that girdeth me with strength, and maketh my way perfect. He maketh my feet like hinds' feet, and setteth me upon my high places. He teacheth my hands to war, so that a bow of steel is broken by *mine arms. Thou hast also given me the shield of thy salvation: and thy right hand hath holden me up, and thy gentleness hath made me great. Thou hast enlarged my steps under me that my feet did not slip"* (Ps. 18:27-36).

Many years ago, I stood in the office of President Ronald Reagan. On his desk was a plaque that read, "A man can become too big in his own eyes to be used by God, but never too small." In the midst of unrelenting opposition, David was able to accomplish great things for his King, because he stayed humble…small in his own eyes. So can you. David knew that the key to success was to obey Jehovah, the true kingmaker.

When his enemies attacked David, he had a choice…to curse or reverse. You and I have that same choice. When we reverse, we back into the arms of Jesus for *"the eternal God is thy refuge, and underneath are the everlasting arms"* (Deut. 33:27, KJV).

David prayed to the eternal God, *"for by you I can run through a troop…"* (Ps. 18:29, NKJV). That was an impossible feat for man, but not for God.

When Israel was at war with the Philistines, three of David's brothers became soldiers in King Saul's army. David arrived in camp only to be rejected by his brothers. "I know your pride and the insolence of your heart," they scoffed (1 Sam. 17:28, NKJV). He was rejected by King Saul, who said "You are just a boy. You are not able to go against this man of war" (see 1 Sam. 17:33). But David refused to be distracted. He got his eyes on the King of kings, and would not surrender the leadership of his life to Saul, to his brothers, or even to Goliath's humiliating words: "Am I a dog, that you come to me with sticks?" (1 Sam. 17:43, NKJV)

None of these could discourage David with God as his source. He hung onto his dream. The degree of opposition it takes to discourage a true warrior will determine whether he is destined for the pit or the palace. David was willing to pay any price...face any opposition...for he knew that his victory was God's victory. His victory was a victory for his family, his seed, and his nation. David's destiny was defined by his determination and every decision he made in battle. And so is yours!

David believed he would be king when no one else acknowledged his anointing. Your perceptions of yourself will determine the possibilities you pursue. To those around David, he was a shepherd boy with a rawhide sling. To David, his sling was the priceless, bejeweled sword of a warrior king. Others saw only David's rags; but in David's own eyes, he was robed with the majesty befitting a king.

God was David's shield. He knew his feet would not slip because his eyes were fixed on the Lord. His hands were the callused hands of a shepherd, but they held firmly to the hand of the Eternal One. One word from God changed his life forever. Our circumstances are always subject to change, if God arms us with strength and power.

The trials David faced did not matter. He knew he was destined not for the pit, but for the palace...not for disgrace, but for dignity. When you and I put our hands in His hands, he makes our hands to war with shouts of victory. Rejoice! For the shield of your salvation, the King of kings and Lord of lords, Jesus Christ, is leading you. You are truly under divine appointment.

Bridge-Building

"Pray for the peace of Jerusalem…" (Ps. 122:6).

Many have asked about the bridge of love between Christians and Jews that I suggested to Prime Minister Begin. We have been building bridges of love ever since that first meeting in 1980. We are now building the greatest bridge of our lives. It is called the Jerusalem Prayer Team. The mayor of Jerusalem launched it in Dallas, Texas on June 9, 2002. Mayor Ehud Olmert said, "I wish to thank you on behalf of the people of Jerusalem for your support, for your care, for your love, for your friendship, for your generosity. I will go back…to Jerusalem, and I will tell the people of Jerusalem that we have established here in Dallas something that will spread across America, and later across the world…the Jerusalem Prayer Summits…the Jerusalem Prayer Team…that I have the honor to inaugurate today. I promised it to my friend, Mike Evans, that I would join him in going from one congregation to the other, from one community to the other, to participate in the Jerusalem Prayer Summits. And we will talk, and we will approach people, and we will share with them the responsibility and the love that Christians and Jews have together for the destiny of Jerusalem. For the future of Jerusalem, for the love of God for this city, for the love of God for all of us, thank you, thank you from Jerusalem. God bless all of you!"

September 11, 2001 was a tragic day in American history. It was a physical manifestation of a battle that had been lost weeks, months, and possibly years before because of a lack of prayer. Osama bin Laden had attacked America for years, but the church was asleep. The demonic powers that influenced him need to be violently confronted by holy angels on assignment through the power of prayer—as in the time of Daniel.

I am certain God has raised up Nehemiahs and Esthers to do just that—not only to pray the Prayer of David, but to be the Prayer of David to the suffering house of Israel.

The vision of the Jerusalem Prayer Team is to have one million intercessors praying daily for national revival according to Second Chronicles 7:14, as prophesied by King David's son, Solomon. Also pray the prayer of King David, who declared: *"Pray for the peace of Jerusalem; they shall prosper that love thee"* (Ps. 122:6, KJV). Praying for the peace of Jerusalem is not praying for stones or dirt. They don't weep or bleed. It is praying for God's protection over the lives of the citizens of Jerusalem. It is praying for revival. It is praying for God's grace to be poured out.

The pastor of Corrie ten Boom's grandfather went to him and told him that his church was going to pray for the peace of Jerusalem. It inspired the ten Boom family to begin praying weekly. As the chairman of the board of Corrie ten Boom House in Haarlem, Holland, we have made the decision to revive this hundred-year-old prayer tradition. We are asking for one million Christians to join the Jerusalem Prayer Team, and are asking one hundred thousand churches to begin praying weekly during their Sunday services for the peace of Jerusalem.

Would you become a Jerusalem Prayer Team member, and would you encourage others to do so? You can email us at jpteam@sbcglobal.net, or write to: The Jerusalem Prayer Team, P.O. Box 910, Euless, TX 76039.

Since the turn of the city, there have been five thousand terrorist attacks in the Bible land. There have been more suicide bombings in the city of Jerusalem than in any other city in the world. David faced his giant and said, *"Is there not a cause?"* (1 Sam. 17:29, KJV)

The events of September 11th were no accident. In Isaiah 14:13, satan challenged God with "I will sit also upon the mount of the congregation, in the sides of the north" (KJV). This is the Temple site. Satan's last threat to God was that he would sit on the Temple site on the side of the north and do battle against God. The result of this battle is the devastation to the city of Jerusalem, the rage that is being manifested in Judea and Samaria, and the attack on America. Nehemiah saw the fire burning in Jerusalem and said, *"When I heard these words, I sat down and wept and mourned certain days, and fasted and prayed before the God of Heaven"* (Neh. 1:4, KJV).

As I write this book, I know how Nehemiah felt. I fasted and prayed sixty-one days for God to answer my prayers and the prayers of the children of Jerusalem...Jewish, Christian, and Arab alike. The nations of the world cannot solve the problem of Jerusalem; they have tried. I am sure that is one of the reasons I wrote this book. I prayed the Prayer of David in Jerusalem, asking God to answer my prayer.

I prayed that God would send a shield of protection over the city of Jerusalem, over the Bible land, and over America. I prayed that God would send revival to both nations. I will continue to pray this prayer daily according to Psalms 20.

The House of Israel is in a state of terror, as are all the children of the Bible land. They need the Lord to answer them in their day of terror. They need the God of Jacob to defend them. They need help from the sanctuary, and strength out of Zion. Now you know my prayer, and when it began. I believe one million intercessors praying daily and one hundred thousand churches praying weekly for the peace of Jerusalem will move heaven and earth. Heaven and earth met in Jerusalem, and they will meet there again. The command and control center for the spiritual warfare affecting the world is not in Baghdad. It is, in fact, Jerusalem. That is where Satan said he would mount his battle against God. (Isaiah 14:13)

The most important words of Jesus are found in the Great Commission. It declares that Christians be a witness unto Him in Jerusalem, Judea, Samaria, and the uttermost parts of the earth. The truth is that the church was birthed in Jerusalem, but has not been a witness unto Jesus in Jerusalem, Judea and Samaria. The church has not emulated the love that Corrie ten Boom manifested. You and I must humble ourselves, pray, and stand in the gap. This is not an appeal to judge the church, but simply to say, "Lord, this is me in need of prayer."

If you will pray daily, if you will be a part of the Lord's answering this prayer, and a part of touching the destiny of the City of David, then contact me at The Jerusalem Prayer Team, P.O. Box 910, Euless, TX 76039.

The Corrie ten Boom House in Haarlem, Holland is the center for the Jerusalem Prayer Team in that nation. From there, churches of all nations are being encouraged to pray every Sunday for the peace of Jerusalem. A prayer meeting to pray for the peace of Jerusalem is held every day in the ten Boom home, fulfilling her grandfather's burden.

Amazingly, the ten Boom family prayed Psalms 20 for protection. Corrie would say to the Jews in the hiding place, "Don't worry, angels are around this house. You may not see them, but they are there, protecting you." Not one Jewish person they protected was caught…even the ones in the hiding place escaped after the Nazis came to arrest the ten Boom family.

Over the years, a great number of Jews were hidden in the clock shop, many for just a few days as they headed for Palestine to escape Hitler's ovens. When the Gestapo (the German secret police) raided the house, the entire ten Boom family was taken prisoner.

"It was the last time the ten Boom family would be together…Opa, his children, and one grandson. One hundred years before, almost to the day, in 1844, his father had started a prayer group for the 'peace of Jerusalem.' And now, here they were, arrested for *Judenhilfe*, helping Jewish people escape Nazi persecution and death." (*Return to the Hiding Place*, Hans Poley, p. 147. Mr. Poley was the first person hidden by the ten Boom family.)

Casper (84), Betsie (59), and Christiaan (24) died as prisoners. Corrie suffered through prison, but, through a miracle, lived to tell the story. Four Jews who were secreted in the hiding place were never caught. They miraculously escaped to safety. Even though the Nazis knew they were there, they couldn't find them.

One of the four was a Jewish rabbi who vowed that he would come back and sing the praises of God. On June 28, 1942, the ten Boom family took him into their home. His name was Meijer Mossel. He was the cantor of the Jewish community in Amsterdam. He told the ten Booms, "I am a *chazzen* [cantor]. Where is my Torah? Where is my shul [synagogue]? Where is my congregation? The goyim [Gentiles] have laid it all to waste. They have come for the Children of Zion! My only purpose in life is to sing praises to Adonai, the Lord. I am a Yehude, a Yid [one who praises Adonai]."

In March 1974, he went to Corrie ten Boom's room, and, with tears of joy streaming down his face, sang to the Almighty in Hebrew. The rabbi's life had been saved through the power of prayer. To his amazement, Corrie walked into the clock shop. She smiled at him as he walked downstairs. She had just returned from the filming of the Billy Graham movie *The Hiding Place*.

For approximately one hundred years, from 1844 to 1944, the ten Booms conducted meetings to "pray for the peace of Jerusalem." It is amazing that told me eighteen years ago to restore the clock shop. To think that the Lord finally got through my thick skull that prayer is the key...and ONLY prayer.

Mother Teresa was one of the first people to tell me she would pray daily for the peace of Jerusalem in Rome according to Psalms 122:6. She said to me, "Love is not something you say; it's something you do." I believe that with all my heart. That is why I am appealing to you to join me in seeing what King David saw…what Solomon saw…and what our beloved Lord saw as they prayed in Jerusalem. Each experienced the power of God in Jerusalem—God's glory filled the houses where they stood!

As you and I pray the Prayer of David, it is my prayer that His glory will fill the house again!

David had the most amazing track record for getting his prayers answered! He was simply praying a "God prayer" that you, too, can pray. He believed it; you can, too!

1. Join me in praying this wonderful Prayer of David…daily!

2. I have a calendar that I mark with "PDV" (Prayer of David Victory) every day as I pray. Some days, I mark an "SFH" (safe from harm), "RMG" (remember my gifts), "GMHD" (grant my hearts desires), or "ALMP" (Lord answer all my prayers) next to "PDV."

3. I have made this prayer into a card to fit in my wallet. Every time I open my wallet, I want God to bless my giving! I would be glad to send you one of these cards. (May He remember all of my gifts.)

4. *Reread this little book once a week during the next month.* This prayer is a revelation. You may have it, but **until it has you**, coronation day will not come.

5.   Personalize the prayer. (Insert your name into the prayer, and pray it in faith.) I am more convinced of Christ's existence than my own. This prayer is God's word. When Jesus appeared to me, I bought a Bible. It said the Word of God, but I changed it to the words of God. These are His words from Heaven to earth. It's time we put more faith in them than in our circumstances. I have seen kings, prime ministers, and presidents greatly honored. However, once you honor the Word of God, and give it the highest priority in your life, your faith will grow, and you will outlast the adversaries of your soul. No matter what comes your way—hell or high water—you will fulfill your destiny.

6.   Expect a miracle. When the mail comes, say to yourself, "Is that my miracle?" When the phone rings say, "Is that my miracle?"

7.   Find a prayer partner who will agree with you. Visit with your prayer partner weekly and discuss this prayer together.

8.   Start teaching it in your Sunday school class. If you're a pastor, be my guest and preach it as a series. If you have a Bible study, share it there. For a simple start, tell your friends. Your brain believes what you say much more than what anyone else says.

9. Start praying it over America, over Israel, your family and loved ones...and of course yourself.

10. Make the Prayer of David the final word in your life! Stand on it, meditate on it! See it happening. Reject everything that does not line up with this Word.

11. Bind satan when he tells you God will not answer. In the natural course of things, David should never have had his prayers answered, but he did.

I began this book in the city of David, and almost exactly one year later, I ended it there. David received one word from God through the prophet Samuel that changed his life forever. One word from God will also change your life forever. If we don't get in *the* Word, we will not receive *a* word. I pray that you will spend at least fifteen minutes each day in God's word. Read all of the Psalms of David. There are some powerful gems that the Lord wants to leave with you.

The first psalm I read was Psalms 1. I memorized it and meditated on it daily. David declared that if we would meditate on God's word day and night, whatsoever we did would prosper. I have meditated on the Word for forty-three years now. It will surely cure meditating on regrets. King David refused to mope in the ashes of defeat. Many Christians are bound by a slave mentality—meditating on defeat and failure. Once you make up your mind that there is a greater King than David—the King of kings and Lord of lords—and that He has a divine plan for your life, His Word will be the final word. Begin meditating on that Word, and nothing will be able to stop you from your destiny. You will develop a warrior mentality.

I end this book with a prayer of agreement for you, dear reader, that you will now make a life-changing God-connection by believing the Prayer of David and allowing the power of the Word to become an unquenchable fire in your soul.

The Prayer of David

"In times of trouble, may the Lord respond to your cry. May the God of Israel keep you safe from all harm. May He send you help from His sanctuary and strengthen you from Jerusalem. May He remember all your gifts and look favorably on your burnt offerings. May He grant your heart's desire and fulfill all your plans! May we shout for joy when we hear of your victory, flying banners to honor our God. May the Lord answer all your prayers" (Ps. 20:1-6, NLT).

Whom can he trust? To whom can he tell his most intimate frustrations? Where can the king rest his weary spirit?

Suddenly he jumps to his feet with hands lifted to heaven, and bellows out, "In your day of trouble, may the God of Jacob keep you from all harm. May He send you aid from His sanctuary in Zion. May He remember with pleasure the gifts you have given Him, your sacrifices and burnt offerings. May He grant you your heart's desire and fulfill all your plans! May there be shouts of joy when we hear of your victory, flying flags with praise to God for all that He has done for you. May He answer all your prayers!"

As David finishes his prayer, he looks eastward. The enemy is running in panic; they have left everything. He hears a mighty sound and turns around to see the entire nation rushing to the defense of their king...blowing trumpets of praise and flying banners of victory with the names of God blowing in the wind.

About the Author

❧

Rev. Michael Evans is a *Time Magazine* best-selling author. He has written seventeen books. His three latest books include: The Prayer of David: In Times of Trouble, The Unanswered Prayer of Jesus, and Why Christians Should Support Israel are available in local bookstores, or by contacting his office.

Rev. Evans has appeared on BBC, the *Good Morning Show* in London, *Good Morning America*, *Nightline*, and *Crossfire*. His articles have been published in newspapers throughout the world, including the *Wall Street Journal*, and the *Jerusalem Post*.

He has been a confidante to most of Israel's prime ministers, and to both of Jerusalem's mayors. He is the recipient of numerous awards, including the distinguished Ambassador Award by the State of Israel.

Rev. Evans is a dynamic speaker who has spoken at more than 4000 churches, and in 41 stadiums worldwide. His voice has been heard from the Royal Palace in Madrid to the Kremlin Palace in Moscow. He has been on the cutting-edge of events in Israel for more than two decades...from the state funeral of Yitzchak Rabin to the signing of the Peace Accords in 1993, and the 43rd General Assembly of the United Nations in Geneva.

In addition, Mr. Evans hosts prayer summits in local churches throughout the world with national and international leaders. The Honorable Ehud Olmert, former mayor of Jerusalem, and now Vice Premier of Israel, and former Prime Minister Benjamin Netanyahu are personal friends of Rev. Evans, and strong supporters of the Jerusalem Prayer Team. Mr. Evans' wife, Carolyn, is the founder of the Christian Woman of the Year Association. This organization has presented awards to such notable women as Ruth Graham, Elizabeth Dole, Mother Teresa, Vonette Bright, Didi Robertson, and Shirley Dobson.

Mike and Carolyn reside in Fort Worth, Texas. They are the parents of four children, Michelle, Shira, Rachel, and Michael David. They have three grand-children, Jason, Ashley and Joshua.

Michael D. Evans
Telephone: (817) 268-1228
FAX: (817) 285-0962
Email: jpteam@sbcglobal.net

Prayers of David

(All scriptures are New International Version)

PSALM 142
A prayer when he was in the cave.

I cry aloud to the LORD; I lift up my voice to the LORD for mercy. I pour out my complaint before him; before him I tell my trouble.

When my spirit grows faint within me, it is you who know my way. In the path where I walk men have hidden a snare for me. Look to my right and see; no one is concerned for me. I have no refuge; no one cares for my life.

I cry to you, O LORD; I say, "You are my refuge, my portion in the land of the living." Listen to my cry, for I am in desperate need; rescue me from those who persue me, for they are too strong for me. Set me free from my prison, that I may praise your name.

Then the righteous will gather about me because of your goodness to me.

PSALM 3:5-6

I lie down and sleep; I wake again, because the LORD sustains me. I will not fear the tens of thousands drawn up against me on every side.

PSALM 17:8,15

8. Keep me as the apple of your eye; hide me in the shadow of your wings from the wicked who assail me, from my mortal enemies who surround me.

15. And I-in righteousness I will see your face; when I awake, I will be satisfied with seeing your likeness.

PSALM 18:2, 28-29

2. The LORD is my rock, my fortress and my deliverer; my God is my rock, in whom I take refuge. He is my shield and the horn [1] of my salvation, my stronghold.

28-29. You, O LORD, keep my lamp burning; my God turns my darkness into light. With your help I can advance against a troop; with my God I can scale a wall.

PSALM 19:14

May the words of my mouth and the meditation of my heart be pleasing in your sight, O Lord, my Rock and my Redeemer.

PSALM 20:7

Some trust in chariots and some in horses, but we trust in the name of the LORD our God.

PSALM 23:4

Even though I walk through the valley of the shadow of death, I will fear no evil, for you are with me; your rod and your staff, they comfort me.

PSALM 27:4

One thing I ask of the LORD, this is what I seek: that I may dwell in the house of the LORD all the days of my life, to gaze upon the beauty of the LORD and to seek him in his temple.

PSALM 28:7

The LORD is my strength and my shield; my heart trusts in him, and I am helped. My heart leaps for joy and I will give thanks to him in song.

PSALM 30:5

For his anger lasts only a moment, but his favor lasts a lifetime; weeping may remain for a night, but rejoicing comes in the morning.

PSALM 34:4, 7-10

4. I sought the LORD , and he answered me; he delivered me from all my fears.

7-10: The angel of the LORD encamps around those who fear him, and he delivers them. Taste and see that the LORD is good; blessed is the man who takes refuge in him. Fear the LORD , you his saints, for those who fear him lack nothing. The lions may grow weak and hungry, but those who seek the LORD lack no good thing.

PSALM 37:37

Consider the blameless, observe the upright; there is a future for the man of peace.

PSALM 40:2-3

He lifted me out of the slimy pit, out of the mud and mire; he set my feet on a rock and gave me a firm place to stand. He put a new song in my mouth, a hymn of praise to our God. Many will see and fear and put their trust in the LORD.

PSALM 46:1-2

God is our refuge and strength, an ever-present help in trouble. Therefore we will not fear, though the earth give way and the mountains fall into the heart of the sea.

PSALM 91:1, 2, 10, 11, 15

1-2: He who dwells in the shelter of the Most High will rest in the shadow of the Almighty. I will say of the LORD , "He is my refuge and my fortress, my God, in whom I trust."

10-11: Then no harm will befall you, no disaster will come near your tent. For he will command his angels concerning you to guard you in all your ways;

15. He will call upon me, and I will answer him; I will be with him in trouble, I will deliver him and honor him.

PSALM 92:10

You have exalted my horn like that of a wild ox; fine oils have been poured upon me.

PSALM 119:114

You are my refuge and my shield; I have put my hope in your word.

Timely, Live Radio Program Begins Broadcasts from Jerusalem

"Jerusalem Prayer Report" To Provide News, Prayer Focus

JERUSALEM, March 20, 2003 – The Jerusalem Prayer Team, a massive prayer movement committed to praying for Israel and the peace of Jerusalem, has released a new, 60-second radio program that focuses on breaking news and prayer needs in Israel.

The program, called "Jerusalem Prayer Report," is broadcast live six days a week. It provides a daily update of war- and military-related activities in Israel as well as areas of prayer need.

"This program provides breaking news from Israel to Christians throughout the United States," said Michael David Evans, founder of the Jerusalem Prayer Team and the Corrie Ten Boom Foundation. "Reports like this help Christians better know how to pray for the Jewish people – which is vital," he said.

The "Jerusalem Prayer Report" is delivered live daily at 5 am EST, although radio stations are free to use the program at other times during the day. It is produced and reported by veteran journalist Dave Bender, a former producer for the Jerusalem Post's radio program. The program complements a Jerusalem-based Internet news service already on line at the Jerusalem Prayer Team Web site (www.jpteam.org/news.asp).

The Jerusalem Prayer Team was birthed out of the Corrie Ten Boom clock shop in Holland. The Ten Booms had a 100-year prayer meeting (praying for the peace of Jerusalem) from 1844 to 1944. It ended when they were taken to the Nazi concentration camps, after saving more than 800 Jewish lives.

The goal of the Jerusalem Prayer Team is to enlist a million people in America to pray daily for the peace of Jerusalem. More than 300 national, Christian leaders, such Pat Robertson, Tim LeHaye, Joyce Meyers and Ann Graham Lotz support the JPT. The team is undertaking numerous efforts to show encouragement and love for the Jewish people from the Christian church in America.

The JPT receives no funding from the State of Israel, nor does the Jerusalem Prayer Team believe that God loves Arabs in the Bible land any less than He loves the Jews.

The "Jerusalem Prayer Report" is available to all Christian radio stations at no charge and is being syndicated through Renaissance Communications, Inc. For access to the report, go to www.jpteam.org/radio.asp.